ASTRONAUT ELLISON S. ONIZUKA SPACE CENTER

P.O. BOX 833 ▪ KAILUA-KONA, HAWAII 96745 ▪ PHONE 808-329-3441 ▪ FAX 808 326-9751

A MESSAGE TO THE FUTURE GENERATIONS:

*"IF I CAN IMPRESS UPON YOU ONLY ONE IDEA...
LET IT BE THAT THE PEOPLE WHO MAKE THIS
WORLD RUN, WHOSE LIVES CAN BE TERMED
SUCCESSFUL, WHOSE NAMES WILL GO DOWN
IN THE HISTORY BOOKS, ARE NOT THE CYNICS,
THE CRITICS, OR THE ARMCHAIR QUARTERBACKS.*

*THEY ARE THE ADVENTURISTS, THE EXPLORERS,
AND DOERS OF THIS WORLD. WHEN THEY SEE A
WRONG OR PROBLEM, THEY DO SOMETHING ABOUT
IT. WHEN THEY SEE A VACANT PLACE IN OUR
KNOWLEDGE, THEY WORK TO FILL THAT VOID.*

*RATHER THAN LEANING BACK AND CRITICIZING
HOW THINGS ARE, THEY WORK TO MAKE THINGS
THE WAY THEY SHOULD BE. THEY ARE THE
AGGRESSIVE, THE SELF-STARTERS, THE INNOVATIVE,
AND THE IMAGINATIVE OF THIS WORLD.*

*EVERY GENERATION HAS THE OBLIGATION TO FREE
MEN'S MINDS FOR A LOOK AT NEW WORLDS...TO
LOOK OUT FROM A HIGHER PLATEAU THAN THE LAST
GENERATION.*

*YOUR VISION IS NOT LIMITED BY WHAT YOUR EYE
CAN SEE, BUT BY WHAT YOUR MIND CAN IMAGINE.
MANY THINGS THAT YOU TAKE FOR GRANTED WERE
CONSIDERED UNREALISTIC DREAMS BY PREVIOUS
GENERATIONS. IF YOU ACCEPT THESE PAST
ACCOMPLISHMENTS AS COMMONPLACE THEN
THINK OF THE NEW HORIZONS THAT YOU CAN
EXPLORE.*

*FROM YOUR VANTAGE POINT, YOUR EDUCATION
AND IMAGINATION WILL CARRY YOU TO PLACES
WHICH WE WON'T BELIEVE POSSIBLE.*

*MAKE YOUR LIFE COUNT – AND THE WORLD WILL BE
A BETTER PLACE BECAUSE YOU TRIED."*

ELLISON S. ONIZUKA
1980

ELLISON S. ONIZUKA
A Remembrance

ELLISON S. ONIZUKA
A Remembrance

Written by
Dennis M. Ogawa and Glen Grant

Designed by
Bill Fong and Leo Gonzalez

Photographic Contributions by
Noel Black

Published jointly for The Onizuka Memorial
Committee by David Rick/Signature
Publishing
and Bennett Hymer/Mutual Publishing.

First Edition, September 1986
Second Edition, November 1986
Third Edition, April 1987

Library of Congress catalogue card
number 86-062278
ISBN: 0-935180-55-9

Printed and bound in Japan

Table of Contents

Foreword

Throughout the history of human exploration run two common denominators: a vision, and a fierce dedication to fulfilling that vision. Exploring space has been our greatest dream and challenge. And in just 25 years, we have traveled from tentative ventures into the solar system to the bold reaches of the universe.

Space travel challenges the pioneer spirit and inspires the dedication of modern-day trailblazers—the astronaut corps of NASA. These men and women accept the risks because they see the promise of space, of new knowledge about ourselves and our planet, of new technologies that hold the solution to many of earth's problems. These men and women are today's heroes.

This book is about one of these heroes: Ellison Onizuka, a Japanese-American whose dream was to be an astronaut. It starts with Ellison as a child growing up in the coffee fields of Kona, Hawaii, and follows through to the day he lost his life when the space shuttle Challenger exploded on January 28, 1986, just seconds after launch. It is a tribute to a man who inspired others with his humility, his dedication to a cause, and his absolute belief in serving his country.

A month before Ellison died, he expressed his belief in this message he wrote for local Boy Scouts: "The need is great for men who hold high values, such as 'duty to God and country' and 'duty to others.'"

The employees of United Airlines are proud to pay tribute to this man, not because he was unlike other men, but precisely because he was an ordinary man who had a fierce dedication to fulfilling a vision.

James J. Hartigan
President and Chief Executive Officer

UNITED AIRLINES

Mahalo

The Onizuka Memorial Committee would like to extend its sincere appreciation to the many individuals and organizations that contributed to the making of this book.

To United Airlines we extend a special "THANK YOU" for the generous support provided throughout this project and the initial funding which made this book possible.

To Liberty House and The Honolulu Advertiser our gratitude for your generous help in distributing and publicizing the book.

To Aloha Airlines our thanks for the many courtesies extended to the Onizuka committee.

To NASA our thanks for providing information, photographs and personnel assistance.

To Kapiolani Community College, Office of Community Services thank you for providing their excellent computer facilities which eased the cumbersome typing process of writing a book.

To Nippon Golden Network thank you for the use of office space and equipment as well as the untiring help of their secretary, Eunice Nakasone.

To our publishers David Rick and Bennett Hymer who have created and produced this project on behalf of the committee—thank you.

To the writers—Dennis Ogawa and Glen Grant, to the Art Directors —Bill Fong and Leo Gonzalez, and to the photographer—Noel Black our "MAHALO" for your creative talents.

Finally, we must thank the people of Kona who shared their homes and hospitality with the writers and artists so that in turn we may bring Ellison's triumphs and tragedy to light. In the process, we hope we have all done them honor and have passed on to our grandchildren the memory of our astronaut.

The Challenger, cloaked in coastal fog, is readied for its maiden flight. (NASA)

Introduction

The Pacific swells drifted lazily against the lava seawall at Napoʻopoʻo. Across Kealakekua Bay stood a slim white spire, the memorial to Captain James Cook.

I could imagine his ship rocking at anchor. Cook the navigator, the explorer, the map-maker. Cook, who on his three great voyages had charted New Zealand's North and South Island; circled and sought, but never found, Antarctica; explored the Bering Straits; and "discovered" these Hawaiian Islands that the Polynesians had found many centuries earlier. Cook, who admired these islands so much, lost his life at the hands of natives here on this very shore.

A breeze wafted down the hillside behind me. The gentle Kona slope extended upward and upward, past the coffee bushes, past the belt road, beyond the ranches on the higher slopes, and into the clouds. I could see rain showers… and half a rainbow. I knew this mountain. The part I couldn't see would extend above the tops of the clouds like an iceberg piercing arctic whitecaps.

The top of a mountain is a particularly desirable location to view the heavens. Furthermore, a near-equatorial location affords the advantage of viewing the entire celestial sphere. It is not surprising, then, to find a fine astronomical observatory atop Mauna Kea.

Astronomy was the keystone on which the space age was built. Hawaii, however, has played much more than an observer's role. Radar tracking, communications and telemetry were conducted from a station on the rim of Kauai's Waimea Canyon during the Mercury and Gemini flights. The Apollo lunar expeditions returned to earth in Hawaiian waters. And those who would explore the lunar surface would come to learn the ways and the secrets of the volcano here on the slopes of Mauna Loa.

It is not surprising that a boy raised overlooking the anchorage of Captain Cook would have latent interests in exploring. Ellison Onizuka grew up in the morning shadow of the great mountain. He watched the majestic passage of the planets through the ecliptic overhead. Inspired by engineering and by flight, he prepared himself to participate in the excitement of this changing world. And participate he did.

Like Captain James Cook, Lt. Colonel Ellison Onizuka had his life cut short for reasons he could not control. Yet during his years, he accomplished much more than most. Our world is a better place for his being here. He will always be remembered. This is his story.

11 | Neil A. Armstrong

The Star Voyager with the Winning Smile

W
hat makes human beings desire to go to the stars? What makes them leave the safety of earth to penetrate the clouds and orbit in weightlessness hundreds of miles above the land where they were created?

Flying to the moon, the planets and stars is well beyond most of us. In our lifetimes we can only wonder and imagine what future generations will one day take for granted. Yet there are those among us who have not waited for the future. These star voyagers, driven by dreams and passions and courage unknown to the earthbound, have already stepped into the world of tomorrow. While our sights are limited to the horizon, they have seen our planet as a massive, blue orb of sea spinning in the vastness of space. They have felt the exhilaration of lift-off, catapulting to a region where gravity finds new definition.

We still find great comfort in the truism that "what goes up, must come down." And while for us the moon is as intangible as a theatrical paper prop, some of the adventurers have done the unbelievable. They have walked on that distant mass, erected upon it their nation's flag and brought home some of its rocks.

For all these things, we rightfully call them heroes.

At 8:23 a.m. on January 28, 1986, seven of our star voyagers left their launch pad quarters at Cape Canaveral, Florida to board the space shuttle Challenger. This massive, white orbiter was a highly sophisticated and complex piece of aerodynamic machinery that had already been launched nine times into "outer space." For most of us, these launchings had almost become routine and the buoyant smiles of the voyagers confirmed that confidence. The video picture is still frozen in our minds, our last glimpse of a team that was as diverse and winning as the spirit of America itself. It was thumbs up.

This is the story of one of those star voyagers. He's the one with the smile that stretches from ear to ear—his eyes still twinkling with a touch of boyish charm and mischief. He is the one who is waving to us as if he knows us. Not to say goodbye, but "I'll see you later," as if he were going fishing down at the beach.

He's the one who grew up on the mauka side of Kona, who was just one of the boys but excelled at most everything he did.

He always made his family proud.

He's the one who was the explorer scout with the clean, pressed uniform and the smart salute who earned his eagle rank by hard work and drive. But he was not straight-laced. He also possessed human frailties with his pranks and

CHAPTER ONE
Voyagers to Distant Lands

The island of Hawaii as viewed from space.
(NASA)

Ellison Onizuka's grandparents never dreamed of flying to the stars. They were just simple Japanese farmers who never had such foolish thoughts. But Kichihei Onizuka and his wife Wakano were among those Japanese voyagers who in the late 1890's dreamed of a new life in an unknown land called Hawaii. There are no records to tell us why they decided to leave their small village of Minou, in the forest highlands of the prefecture of Fukuoka. Yet the reasons must have been compelling—in those days, one did not simply walk off the farm for a better life. A family belonged to the land just as surely as *kami* or spirits, belonged to every living and inanimate object. Generations of Onizukas had lived in Minou—at Takami in Ukiha-machi, a family tomb still stands as a proud symbol of their ancient ancestral roots. The Onizuka clan had produced for hundreds of years a successive line of simple farmers, foresters, tradesmen and, as genealogy shows, at least one powerful shogun.

For Kichihei and Wakano to have decided to sever their ties with this heritage—even for a temporary time—required an act of courage. Perhaps poor crops had driven them away—a drought may have cracked and shrunk the land or like hundreds of small villages, Minou may have suffered from political unrest in the turbulent years of the Meiji Era. Leaflets about the riches to be made in America or Hawaii, lands known as "heaven" by the common folk, may have also lured the young couple to the adventure in a distant land. Whatever their specific reasons, the young couple were leaving an old, certain world to courageously face the challenge of surviving in a land where clothing, language, lettering, food, housing and lifestyle would all be alien.

Kichihei and Wakano arrived on the island of Oahu and began working in the sugar plantation fields. But life on the Hawaiian sugar plantation was tedious, back-breaking and unrewarded. They soon left Oahu and searched for something better in the rural district of Kona on the island of Hawaii. Kona had become, by the turn of the century, a peaceful, remote settlement famous, as world-reknowned Victorian visitor Isabella Bird observed, for "oranges, coffee, pineapples, and silence." Quiet, picturesque churches, a few country stores, scattered ranches and corrals, coffee mills and native grass houses intermingled with wooden frame homes, comprised this outpost of the Pacific. Many of the few remaining native Hawaiians, whose population had been decimated by the horrendous diseases of the modern world, had become *paniolos* or cowboys, for Kona's profitable ranching and sheepherding businesses. The *kamaaina haole*, or longtime white settlers, were the descendants of missionaries, merchants, sailors and adventurers with distinctive names like Paris, Greenwell, Hind and Parker. Although they held social and racial prominence, they too had blended into the distinctive Kona lifestyle. They spoke Hawaiian and pidgin English, shared their produce with their neighbors, knew everyone's name and gossip and used two fingers when they ate their *poi*.

The Kona world into which the Onizukas stepped was a rural haven unlike the sugar plantations. With many of the other Japanese immigrants, they settled away from the arid, hot plains of the coast, preferring the cooler regions of mauka Kona, 1,500 ft. high on the slopes of Mt. Hualalai. In the village of Keopu, Kichihei and Wakano built their home and began a small coffee farm on leased land. Thousands of immigrant, independent farmers such as the Onizukas, were a welcomed boon to the coffee industry. Through their labor, Kona coffee became world famous for its distinctive and highly desired flavor. The entire family, parents and children, worked the arable fields, harvested the beans and on the back of their "Kona nightingales" or donkeys, hauled their produce to the mills. Since they did not work for wages or live under the paternal care of the sugar interests, the coffee farmer was an independent, proud breed of entrepreneur. Labor in the coffee field was no less tiring or relentless than sugar. The chances of a failed crop or dropping food prices were far more risky for the independent farmer. But in their rural isolation and independence, the Japanese of Kona could actually rebuild a way of life that

The West Hawaii coast in the late 19th century was a remote, rural settlement of coffee fields, cowboys, merchants, native Hawaiians and Japanese immigrants. Kawaihae Landing pictured here in 1882 was one of its major ports. (Hawaii State Archives)

resembled the villages they had left behind. The pain of homesickness could be tempered in the comfort of family, religion, community and cultural continuity.

In Kona, the immigrants had sought that continuity by quickly organizing themselves into *kumiai*, or community associations. The *kumi* resembled the organization of the village in Japan where mutual assistance and reciprocal sharing was an integral way of life. If a family needed financial assistance, the first place they sought help was the *kumi*—neighbors often formed a mutual investment and loaning system called *tanomoshi*. Members of the *kumi* also helped each other by helping to build homes, pick crops during the harvest, or in cases of accident or hardship, to provide support. Joyous celebrations were also organized by the *kumi*—births, marriages and the seasonal festivities of New Year's, the Obon, Girl's and Boy's Day, and the Hanamatsuri, or Buddha Day. When Buddhist temples were established in Kona, it was the *kumi* that arranged for ministers to make circuit travels to the more remote areas and promoted Japanese language schools for the proper instruction of its children. During tragedies and deaths, the bereaving family always knew that the necessary arrangements would be made by the *kumi* and a decent reception for mourners would always be prepared.

It was thus a good life for the Onizukas in Kona. As many Japanese leaders in the community were fond of saying, these were the days for *eiju dochaku*, settling roots in the new land. The *kumi* helped stabilize a unique spirit of

Historic Mokuaikaua Church rises above the little village of Kailua in the early 1900's. (Hawaii State Archives)

community among the Japanese. The Buddhist churches uplifted and eased the soul through the perpetration of customs and religious rites. Japanese foodstuffs, sake, newspapers, clothing and household products even found their way to as distant a place as Kona. But it was the birth of the *nisei*, the second generation, that truly signaled the emergence of a permanent family and community.

Kichihei and Wakano had seven children—six sons and one daughter. It was common practice for rural Japanese families to be large and most immigrants continued the tradition in Hawaii. Large numbers of *nisei* created, of course, new needs. Language schools were established for the care and education of the youth as a means to complement their American public school education. Both at home and in the language schools, the *nisei* were instilled with proper family and community values—*on*, or respect; *giri*, or obligation; *enryo*, or holding back; *haji*, or shame; and *yamato damashi*, or pride of ancestry. Within the home, father was the patriarch and master, his often stern and stoic presence an object of reverence. When father demanded his food or sake, the children unquestioningly obeyed. Mother could be equally subdued, but she was invariably softer, her voice more compassionate in her

ABOVE: *Japanese immigrants frequently found employment in the fertile coffee farms of Hawaii. Workers posed on the Olaa Plantation in the early 1900's. (Bishop Museum) RIGHT: The Onizuka coffee farm in mauka Kona.*

Kona Memories

William and Bertha Paris were interviewed at their spacious ranch home in Kainaliu, Kona. Billy Paris is a descendant of missionaries and merchants who settled in the Kona district in the mid-nineteenth century. Bertha is an expressive, amicable Hawaiian woman who speaks nostalgically of visiting the Onizukas in the old days of Kona.

"BILL: We were so proud to see what a fine example he set for the youth. He lifted up our kids. They were at the bottom of the totem pole in their school tests, but after his visit, their scores jumped up twenty points. You can not help but feel there was a motivation he left behind to stimulate these youngsters.

I think they realized that no matter how humble or simple your beginnings, through hard work, desire and determination you can reach your goals. I think that is what he has given them. This was a country boy that went to the top. He did it on his own by determination and application.

BERTHA: Going to the Onizukas was like a reunion. Mrs. Onizuka always brought us ice cream. We'd visit for an hour with Billy swapping news with Mr. Onizuka. We used to share with each other. We'd take a box of Paris mangos and drop them off over there. And when Billy butchered cattle, he'd remember merchants up and down the highway. They were good to us and they took care of the poor cowboys. "Don't worry," they would say, "pay next time." They gave credit. Mr. Spencer, who lives in Kailua, says if it wasn't for the Onizukas, his family would've starved. "They always gave us something. When we could pay, we'd pay." That's the kind of people they were. Ellison came from good stock."

Heiji Yamagata, the issei proprietor of Kona's Yamagata Store, proudly poses with his produce and "Kona nightingale." (Bishop Museum)

guidance and demands. Children were trained to be polite, quiet, obedient and hardworking. And always the values of education and self-improvement were instilled; sacrifices must be made so that successive generations could have the skills and knowledge to bring success to themselves and their offspring.

With the responsibility of a family preoccupying their thoughts, and with so many comforts of the homeland to ease their separation, the idea of returning to Japan became a faded memory for many immigrants. Kona was slowly becoming the new homeland. Their American born, English-speaking children were a constant reminder that their desires for a better life in Hawaii had been fulfilled. The days and weeks accumulated into years and their once firm, youthful bodies had now been aged in the Kona soil. For Kichihei and Wakano, their adventurous voyage to another world must have seemed in retrospect a fortunate decision—just another passage in life's many toils and joys. The satisfaction of achievement replaced in time the thrill of dreaming.

On a clear, still Kona night, the sky blazes with the tiny lights of the universe. Ancient Hawaiians used to watch these stars and note their movements. They gave names to over 150 of them and could guide their sailing by patterns the stars formed in the night sky. The coffee farmers of Kona at the turn of the century probably never knew the stars so well. They certainly never dreamt of flying to them. Earthbound farmers do not dream of such things. Such fantasies have no relevance to producing a good and profitable harvest. Wasting time with such fantasies does not provide your children with an education. Who could believe that human beings would one day fly in the sky under their own propulsion or that one day the moon would be walked on by earthlings? Only a fool would have believed that one day one of their own grandchildren would spin around the planet in a metal machine and then glide back down to safety. It was beyond their dreams, their facts and their knowledge.

OPPOSITE: The Onizukas regularly attended Buddhist services at the Honpa Hongwanji Church in Keopu. LEFT: The Buddhist temple and language school was the cultural center of the Japanese immigrant community. Issei and their nisei children pose before a Kohala language school at the turn of the century. (Bishop Museum) OVERLEAF: "Space is the new ocean and this nation must sail upon it." President John F. Kennedy (NASA)

23

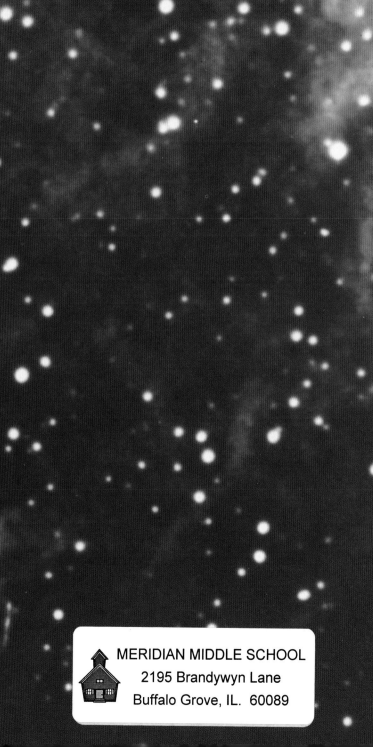

MERIDIAN MIDDLE SCHOOL
2195 Brandywyn Lane
Buffalo Grove, IL. 60089

CHAPTER TWO

On the Shoulders of Giants

Mrs. Mitsue Onizuka, proprietess of the Onizuka Store.

ichihei and Wakano Onizuka kept a very traditional Japanese home in the high country of Kona. So when Ellison's father, Masamitsu, the second son born to Kichihei and Wakano, was ready for marriage, instead of following the American path of romance, his parents encouraged the employment of a traditional *baishakunin*, or matchmaker. Masamitsu was twenty-nine years old when a Kona matchmaker arranged for him to meet and marry a Kona Japanese *nisei* ten years his junior. Mitsue Nagata was the daughter of Mr. and Mrs. Senkichi Nagata, Japanese immigrant coffee farmers who lived south in Kealakekua.

Senkichi had immigrated from Japan with his brother at about the same time as the Onizukas. The two brothers had intended to go to California, but Senkichi decided to remain in Honolulu. At first he found a farming job on Oahu near the Nuuanu Pali. Soon after, he migrated to the Kona coffee fields and was married to a Japanese picture bride. Mitsue was born in mauka Kona at Holualoa before the family moved to Kealakekua. A pretty young girl of nineteen who was not afraid of work and respected the wishes of her parents, she later recalled that she "had to say yes" in the marriage arrangements. In those days, one did not question one's parents.

Even though the marriage had been arranged, the newlyweds soon became a working partnership, carving a distinct life for themselves in pre-World War II Kona. Masamitsu was a good provider, an out-going, friendly man and an active member of the Keopu community. Realizing that his older brother would inherit the coffee lands which his parents now owned and desirous of his own business profession, he obtained a job at Mr. Isamu Ota's grocery store.

Mr. Ota was a well-known Kona general merchandise supplier that operated largely on a credit business. Cowboys, farmers and other families would purchase their foodstuffs, clothing and supplies from Mr. Ota with the promise of payment at payday or harvest. While this system worked fine on the plantation where the resources of the store were backed up by the management, for a private entrepreneur it was a difficult way to survive. Since Kona residents did not have a lot of cash, it seemed the only way to do business.

The cash flow dwindled in the hard, lean years of the depression, especially for small farmers and ranchers in Kona. Tired of the pressures and unpaid credit, Mr. Ota finally decided to close up his business and try his hand at vegetable farming. Realizing that Keopu would be without a merchandise store and careful not to follow in the footsteps of Mr. Ota, Masamitsu was now determined to open his own store on a cash and carry business. On May 5, 1933 Masamitsu and Mitsue Onizuka opened up their general merchandise store. Although the cash sales were smaller than credit sales, it was hard-earned, hand-held cash. Masamitsu and Mitsue woke up at dawn with the farmers so as to be ready to supply their daily needs and stayed open well after dark when they returned from the fields.

In some cases, Masamitsu did extend credit to help out the employees of the larger ranchers. Billy Paris of Puuwaawaa Ranch, for example, remembers the time when the Onizuka store helped out his cowboys so that they did not have to always pay cash for their supplies. The ranch would make good any of the men's debts, but Masamitsu was always a lenient creditor, carrying the men who were short of cash. "I have a great deal of aloha for Mr. Onizuka, " Mr. Paris recalls, "for he was very kind to my ranch people." There are many others living in Kona today who still remember the generosity of the Onizukas—one

BELOW: Along a mauka Kona road in the 1930's. (Hawaii State Archives) OPPOSITE TOP: Eldest daughter, Shirley, with her mother in the City of Refuge, the Kona coast, April 1938. OPPOSITE BOTTOM: Ellison's older sisters, Shirley and Norma. (Onizuka Family) FOLLOWING OVERLEAF: The Onizuka Store, once the hub of Keopu, as it appears today.

did not starve, no matter how poor the times, when the Onizuka store was doing business.

Their kindness to their neighbors was extended with neither fanfare nor conspicuous charity. The Onizukas were far from wealthy folk, since the merchandise business was always very modest. In fact, to supplement their income Masamitsu had some leased coffee acreage under cultivation, helped his parent's and brother's coffee business and even operated one of the only taxi services in mauka Kona. Farmers in those days could not afford their own cars and on Friday afternoons would need a ride to the banks in Kealakekua, several miles to the south, before they closed. So Masamitsu would pack up his car and charge a nominal fee to get the men to the bank. Otherwise they would have had to walk or ride their donkeys to meet the banker's hours. If someone in the village needed to go to Hilo in less than a day, they also sought out Masamitsu.

The road to Hilo was a slow, one lane highway that wound around the island and was a full day's affair. Masamitsu had a number of regular passengers including Mrs. Maude Woods, an elderly lady living in Kohala. He would drive her to Hilo at least once a month. And then there was also the taxiing needs of Dr. Walter James Seymour. He and his wife Sadie lived directly across the way from the Onizuka store and if Dr. Seymour had an emergency and could not start his car, he always called upon Masamitsu's taxi. It was always reliable and ready for call.

The Onizuka store also had one of the few telephones in the district. Consequently, if the outside world wanted to get a message to one of the Keopu residents, the Onizuka store was called. Nearly everyday some long distance call from Hilo or Honolulu for one of their neighbors would come over the line. Mitsue would jot the message down and then diligently have it delivered. It was a service provided free of charge. One did not charge for being a good samaritan to one's neighbors.

It is difficult, perhaps, to find that bucolic simplicity and friendliness in today's modern world. But forty years ago, Kona was still an old world village; although most of the people spoke a different language from one another, they still understood the language of the heart. On a typical Sunday morning, mother and father would load up the family touring car or hitch a wagon and make a call on friends or family up Keopu side. They made sure to bring along some special produce they harvested that week or maybe a side of beef they had butchered and smoked. Maybe the distance was only thirty miles, but it was a full day's journey. At every little store or home along the way, friends would be greeted, food and laughter shared and all the common gossip exchanged.

A Man Who Completed His Dream

*Shirley Matsuoka, Ellison's oldest sister, sometimes reflects on why her
younger brother wanted so badly to go into space. She knew him as the child who
loved to take things apart, to look at the inside of a watch or to take apart his toy.
He was also a determined young man who, once he started a task, made sure it was
accomplished right. Shirley reflects on Ellison while sharing a cup of coffee
with her husband George in their modest Kona home.*

❝ *Ellison was someone who whenever he got into doing something,
he wanted to complete what he was doing. I guess going up there into space
was one of his dreams. But knowing him, getting into space was one of the
things to complete his program. He started it and he wanted to get to the
end of it and complete the program. When he started something he wanted
to make sure that thing was completed and everything done right.
I remember once on memorial day, Ellison and his 4H friends made leis.
He was so careful that they were all perfectly sewn and packed and he took
it himself to wherever it had to go. He was always like that—
he made sure it ended right.* **❞**

TOP: *Masamitsu and Mitsue Onizuka pose at
their kitchen table in 1942 with Norma and
Shirley. ABOVE: Ten month old Ellison in his
stroller, April 1947. (Onizuka Family)*

Everyone knew each other back then and sometimes maybe they knew a little
too much. "Talk story" was a way of life, a means of entertainment and a
bonding of the community.

Sometime near mid-afternoon, as you drove along the Mamalahoa
Highway—a winding two-lane thoroughfare that was the only road connecting
mauka Kona to the outside world—you made certain to stop at the Onizuka
store. Mr. Onizuka would cut open a watermelon or maybe Mrs. Onizuka
would pass out some ice cream. There was a long bench on the front porch
where you spent an hour "talking story." They were friendly folk and always
had a good word for everyone and of course never forgot a name of a relative
or a cousin.

You of course knew their children. The two older daughters, Shirley and Norma, helped their mother around the store while Mr. Onizuka worked on the coffee farm or drove the taxi. And you probably would never forget their two younger boys. The smallest was a little rotund rascal that the sisters often kept "caged" up in a makeshift pen of soda boxes. Claude was a lively youngster who was fond of riding his bicycle onto the road. The other boy was a little older, quieter but just as energetic. Ellison had his moments of prankishness. As he got older, you would sometimes see him hunched over the store counter, his face buried in a book. But like his parents, he was always polite. When you entered the small store he would look up from his reading, greet you by name—he never forgot a name—and *always* addressed his elders with a polite "Mr." and "Mrs."

The folks of Kona watched this distinctive young boy with the shy demeanor and the bright smile grow up. They remember him as the four-year-old toddler who stuffed his pockets with candy from his mother's counter and then stood at the edge of the roadway campaigning for Supervisor Robert Hind. "Vote for Robert Hind" he would shout out to passing motorists, throwing them candy. Mr. Hind's father would visit the store and *always* hug the little child and praise him loudly with a hearty "You're the boy!" Ellison had a way of winning people's hearts.

Kona folks also remember how much the Onizukas' older boy always wanted to have a bicycle. When he finally got one, he had a devil of a time learning how to ride it. Over and over he would try, and again and again he would manage to fall over. Later when the little boy was a man and well-known for taking great rides, the older Kona people would laugh to themselves, remembering how he could not even ride a bicycle. He had a way of making people laugh and feel good about themselves.

The most important thing about the Onizukas' oldest boy was that in almost every way, he was not remembered as being extraordinary or someone special. He was just another Kona boy—maybe distinct in his manners, but what child was not? He was remembered as all children are remembered—each in their own way making mischief or doing something funny. People noted these little things not because the children were unique, but because they were involved in each other's lives. Little Ellison Onizuka was just *there*, just like other children were *there*, so of course he was noted, observed, talked about, cared for and loved. Kona was after all a close-knit family.

Of course the world that lay beyond Kona in the first half of the twentieth century was often far from being peaceful, bucolic or family oriented. As the

TOP: *Eight year old Norma babysits her brother Ellison, May, 1947. ABOVE: Ellison graduates to driving a fire truck at the age of three and a half. (Onizuka Family)*

As the modern world rushed into space and war, Kona maintained the quiet charm of old Hawaii, Keauhou, Kona in the 1930's. (Hawaii State Archives)

Kona people enjoyed the cycles of harvest, built up family businesses, got married, raised children, sold groceries and swapped gossip on the front benches, the rest of the world spun madly into and through space. Nations and cities escalated into massive, human societies where human feeling was subservient to profit, greed, violence and quantity. Two world wars were fought. Dictators with distorted racial theories devastated Europe and Asia. The Japanese homeland went to war with America and the immigrant was caught between love of origins and respect for the land of opportunity. Young Hawaii boys, many recruited from the coffee fields of Kona, were thrust into the world-wide conflicts, sacrificing their lives so that matters of loyalty would forever be laid to rest. Weapons were created so demonic that even remote Kona was no longer safe from the prospects of the fallout.

Human beings had also begun to leave the earth. The Wright Brothers were the first. Their historic controlled flight of a winged aircraft at Kittyhawk, North Carolina in 1903 validated the hope of their generation that space could be conquered. Aviation advancements in the following decades became staggering as aircraft became faster, sleeker and more deadly. The world made heroes of our "flyboys" back then—the greatest being Charles Lindbergh. When Lucky Lindy flew the first solo flight across the Atlantic Ocean in 1927, the boyish, good-looking flyer was heralded as the all-American symbol of a nation's primacy of machines in space.

Rockets that could blast off earth with deadly accuracy were no longer science fiction, but a startling scientific fact. In 1926 the first, hand-built, liquid-fuel test rocket was launched in the backyard of scientist Robert Goddard. Within two decades German technicians had perfected the V-2 rocket which was used with deadly effect in their aerial war with Britain. The spiral of discovery, improvement, retesting and rediscovery was so bewildering that the pace of invention often accelerated well beyond the wisdom to always use the new technology wisely. Rocketry, jet propulsion, lift-off, countdown, mach one, the sound barrier, and breaking the sound barrier were the jargon of a new generation who saw the age-old desire to fly to the stars becoming a real possibility.

None of this had any real effect upon Kona. Travel was still slow and steady along the Mamalahoa Highway. Meeting friends was still more important than the speed of your vehicle or the descent of your projectory. Very few Kona folk broke any sound barriers nor desired to do so. If farmers did not dream of going to the stars, neither did grocery store owners.

But if one of their children should decide to join this mad rush to leave the earth, they would have had the privilege of gaining some very special skills from the earthbound settlers of Kona. They would value hardwork, dedication to a dream and the courage to face a new world with humility, pride and diligence. They would know how to share their knowledge, energy and love with their fellow workers. They would have the gift of patience, despite disappointments and exhausting trials. Most preciously, once they left the confines of our planet, they would have gained the ability to look homeward and see more than a gaseous blue sphere of water. They would see the great human community they knew in Kona.

What better qualities make a star voyager?

Years later, after the first manned flight to another world, space traveler Alan Shepard would say that "It's easy to reach out and touch the moon when you're standing on the shoulders of giants." The little Onizuka boy who could not ride a bicycle without falling off, would one day quote those words in gratitude to the people of Kona. "You are all 'giants,'" he would write. He knew well what he was talking about. For he had climbed up on their shoulders to make his own private dreams come true.

The Onizukas with their sons, November 1952. (Onizuka Family) OVERLEAF: Starship Earth as viewed from Apollo 17 during a lunar flight, December 1972. The entire coastline of Africa is visible as well as the south polar ice cap. The Moon as seen from Apollo 11 during its July 1969 manned flight to that distant orb. On board were astronauts Neil Armstrong, Michael Collins and Edwin E. Aldrin, Jr. (NASA)

35

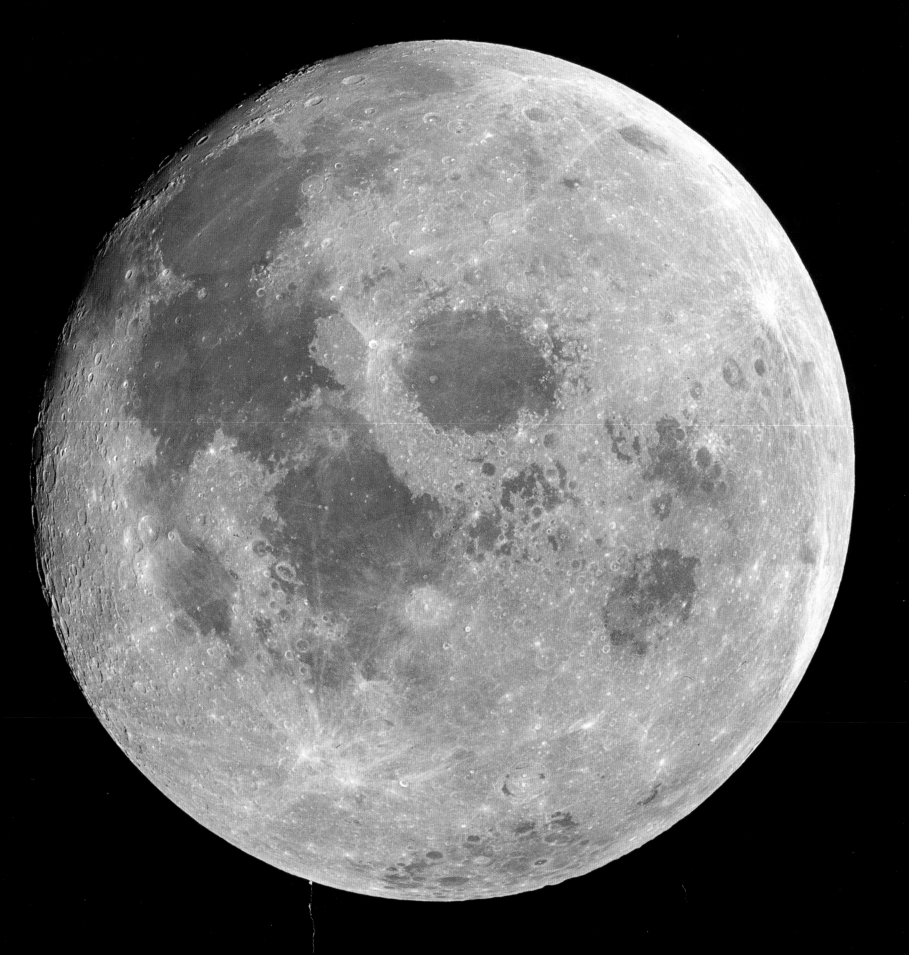

CHAPTER THREE
Outlandish Dreams in Kona

Ellison S. Onizuka, eagle scout. July 26, 1964.
(Onizuka Family)

llison Onizuka, the grandchild of Kona farmers and the first son of Kona grocers, had a dream even as a child that one day he would grow up and become an astronaut. How he got hold of that boyish wish in a world as rural and slow-motion as Kona is anyone's guess. In fact, for those who grew up with him, who knew him and loved him, who had the same experiences as he did and believed they shared even his private thoughts, they too must guess at what motivated this young determined man. For in the years of his boyhood, he never seemed to express any outstanding desires to fly airplanes, walk on the moon or orbit satellites. He was always just one of the boys until the end of his high school days when he suddenly declared that he would be an "engineer." His oldest sister Shirley thought he was talking about locomotive trains.

In the formidable years of Ellison's childhood we see the complexities of the grown adult being shaped. In a sense, the child seems the perfect *mohan seinen*—the model Japanese child who is obedient, quiet, studious, successful and always filial. He excels at all he does, shows restraint and modesty, respects his elders and brings honor to the family name. In school he is a bright, hardworking student who earns good grades. He is not especially creative or artistic—his excellence is in math, common sense knowledge, bookkeeping and science. When he grows up he is bound to be an accountant, a teacher or a doctor. Although respectfully shy when need be, he is not afraid of the crowd. He shows natural leadership ability, enjoys talking in front of large groups, always likes to appear neat and well-groomed. He is elected to school offices, a role he assumes with a serious, parliamentary demeanor. Athletically he is competent, aggressive but not especially gifted. He plays in team sports and eagerly engages in extracurricular activities such as the Boy Scouts and 4-H Clubs. In social situations, specifically dating, he starts going out with girls a little later than the other guys.

In many respects then, young Ellison fit the mold of the *mohan seinen*. But he had other qualities equally as compelling and attractive. His obedience seemed always blended with a certain self-directed stubbornness. Once his mind was made up in a certain direction, even the restraints of family would not often deter him—he sometimes seemed driven by his own private reasons that had little to do with the accolades and honors he earned in the name of his family. Young Ellison also had a temper to complement his determination. You knew he *meant* what he said when he said it. But he was more known by his edge of energetic, good-natured fun and mischief that softened the "egghead" image. His social abilities made it possible for him to function within

a peer group comprised of all types of Kona boys—achievers, athletes, "cruisers"
and the studious. He was remembered as being "quiet," but he was in no way a
loner. He functioned best with his friends, earning distinctions for himself but
never separating himself or rising above those he called his friends. He was a
product of Kona.

Although he was the third child, Ellison was the first son, born June 24,
1946 in the village of Keopu. In Japanese style, the first son is always looked
upon with a little more pride, given more responsibility and also treated with a
little more leniency. The first child, Shirley, was nearly twelve years Ellison's
senior. Norma, the second daughter, was seven years older. Even though they
took care of Ellison and later Claude who was born in 1948, the age differences
between them almost seemed as if there were two different sets of offspring. By
the time Ellison went to high school, Shirley had gotten married and left home

and Norma had moved to Honolulu to go to business college. Ellison and Claude grew up then as two male siblings without too much "interference" from their older sisters.

They did get some "interference" though when they were little. Both Ellison and Claude, Shirley remembers, were curious, energetic boys who could also be "rascals." Ellison was always getting into things, taking household objects or watches apart, finding out how things worked. One New Year's Eve he discovered an unlit roman candle which he took below the house to see how it worked. He had seen the adults light the sticks, so the child set it off with a match. Upstairs loud thumps were vibrating the floor as the candle flared up smoke and explosions. Panicking, the family ran out of the house, rushing downstairs before the "fire" burned down the store. There they discovered that young Ellison had been testing his first rocket.

Boyhood days in Kona during the fifties were largely the same for most of the gang in mauka Kona. "Small kid time" was spent largely playing "cowboys and Indians," shooting marbles, riding bikes and going to school. Ellison and Claude spent a lot of time across the road from the family store at the big lawn of Dr. Seymour. The Seymours had the only lawn in the area and it was perfect for the Onizukas and young Scott and Rusty Seymour to play ball, shoot rubber bands or streams of honohono grass at one another. In the back pig pens they made Fort Apache and refought the Indian Wars over and over again. Big sister Shirley would make the boys Campbell's chicken noodle soup and rice and the Seymour boys were always eager for *musubi* from their Japanese neighbors. Once in awhile Mr. Onizuka opened sodas for the boys and, when time permitted, drove them down to Kailua for swimming in the ocean. Ellison and Claude always loved playing, swimming and fishing in the ocean. "Hey, watch me Dad!," Ellison would shout before he would dive boldly into the water from a rock.

Being the older brother, Ellison had more of the chores to do than Claude and as they got older he'd have to quit playing earlier to go home. He helped out in the store quite a bit and when physically big enough, worked on his father's coffee field. All the children of coffee farmers helped out during the harvest. In fact, Kona schools were the only institutions in the entire Territory of Hawaii that took their vacation in the fall, between August and November. This was to allow the kids to work in the coffee fields. Ellison was not a lazy boy. He did not shy away from work but joined his father diligently in the fields. He also took a job with a small trucking firm run by Mr. Takeo Nagamine and would be seen riding in the back of the truck, helping to unload

deliveries to stores and farms all across the Kona district. Even years later when he came home from college, he went out one morning with his brother and picked five full bags of macadamia nuts, an impressive feat for a boy who had been out-of-shape on the mainland for a year.

As they got older, you could notice the differences between the two boys, especially in school. While Claude was more "laid back" and willing to accept "C's," Ellison had already become an achiever. He worked on his grades to bring home the straight "A" report card and never seemed satisfied unless he had done his very best. During vacation, after picking coffee beans all day, the brothers would play basketball at night. Claude played sports to enjoy himself. Ellison was "real competitive." "When it came to sports," Claude remembers, "he was a master I guess. He did not like to lose."

Ellison's desire to do his best and to pay attention to meticulous detail was also reflected in simple pastimes like model building. Both brothers enjoyed plastic model building, Ellison being especially fond of airplanes and aircraft carriers. When he made a model, it was perfect as specified in the plans. Glue was used sparingly and carefully. Paint was applied with precision, exactly as explained in the directions. And the water-based decals were placed without deviation from the picture on the box. Claude, however, painted his just like he wanted and stuck the decals on where it suited him. When they made sand sliding boards to use on the beach, Ellison's was sanded smooth, nicely colored and resined. Claude's…well, Claude's worked.

Like all brothers who grow up together, they had their moments of sibling rivalry. When the sisters left home, Ellison assumed a certain responsibility for Claude. But like any older brother, it was sometimes embarassing having your kid brother hanging around. So they had their fights. Claude, though, was always huskier than Ellison and despite the age difference had a fighting advantage. Ellison, his mother remembers, would always lose. Their father would pull them apart before they hurt each other and admonish them to make up. "They liked each other," Mrs. Onizuka says with her characteristic understatement. "They were good boys."

Since Ellison excelled at nearly everything he did, it must have been difficult for Claude to always expect the shadow of his brother's limelight. For example, it seemed that Ellison was allowed more leniency than the more free spirited Claude, who was not afraid to play hooky from school and spend his afternoon shooting window panes out of an old deserted building with his BB gun. Both boys got their driver's licenses when they were fifteen and were often given access to their father's car or jeep. Once Ellison raced the family car and

Graduating local style from Honokohau Elementary, 1960. (Onizuka Family)

broke the rear end. He took the car to a mechanic who later showed Mr. Onizuka a hairline crack in the rear end, explaining that sooner or later the accident would have happened. Ellison got away "scot free." A while later, Claude was driving the jeep when the oil pump broke down and the bearings completely burned out. He called the mechanic and told him to tell his father what had happened so that he would not catch hell. It did not matter. When Claude got home, Mr. Onizuka punished him although Ellison had never been scolded for a similar "crime."

Of course Claude had his sweet moments of revenge. For example, there was the time Ellison was going to a prom and had waxed and polished the family car to prime condition. Claude was going to the same dance, so, when Ellison went to shower and get ready, Claude took the car and left his brother stranded. When Ellison got to the prom later, his younger brother judiciously avoided him.

ABOVE: Honors came early to the mohan seinen: a "Speech" medallion and a National Honor Society pin earned in high school.
LEFT: Coming of age in Kona—graduation from Honokohau Elementary in 1960. (Onizuka Family)

43

It was in school, the 4-H Club and scouting that Ellison developed his full potential as an achiever. Both Ellison and Claude attended Honokohau Elementary School and then later Konawaena High School. At Konawaena he participated in a wide variety of extracurricular activities: junior class treasurer, homeroom officer, class paper feature editor, a staff member of the school paper "Wildcat and Quill and Scroll" and a member of the homecoming committee. He was a member of the National Honor Society in both his junior and senior years and played junior and varsity basketball and other intramural sports. In athletics he was perhaps better known as a baseball player. He played for the school team every season from his freshman to his senior year. In 1962 the team went on to become Big Island North Divison champs, a distinction they captured again in 1964 with a 15-0 record. Ellison played center field. In the early sixties, when television had not made an impact in Kona and community activities were full family affairs, everybody went to the ball games. The Onizuka boy stayed in the limelight.

Most Kona youngsters then were joiners of clubs, social organizations or community service groups—you had to be if you expected to have any kind of

Konawaena High School.

fun beyond sports and bike-riding. The clubs provided organized activities, and a chance to meet persons of the opposite sex in chaperoned settings, to travel, learn responsibility and become active members of the community. It was a Kona way of life. So Ellison would not have been alone in his participation in 4-H or scouting. But he did enjoy assuming positions of responsibility. In his sophomore year he was chosen a 4-H treasurer and participated in the annual Ahaolelo or statewide gatherings in Honolulu at the University of Hawaii at Manoa. It was an adventure for the young 4-H members from Kona to travel on their own to Honolulu and visit the "big city." Their trip usually included an excursion to the Bishop Museum where Ellison enjoyed the planetarium. He was also an expert "chicken dresser" who regularly participated in the statewide contest stripping and dressing a chicken for speed. "He was a great chicken stripper," classmate Caroline Nakashima remembers of Ellison. She had met the "quiet and polite" Ellison on their first trip to the 4-H gathering in Honolulu and she was fascinated with his skill at plucking chickens.

One year, Ellison's skill at chicken dressing so outshone the Kona competition, that no 4-H'er bothered to even enter the contest. Worried lest the contest would be cancelled and his chances to go to Honolulu for statewide competitions ruined, Ellison urged Claude to enter the contest. According to his sister Norma, Claude was finally cajoled to give in to Ellison's scheme. He was naturally beaten by his older brother who showed that as casually as he earned his accolades, he always had a purpose.

Keopu had no scouting program. One evening in 1960, Ellison, desirous in his high school years to become involved in scouting, showed up at the basement of a Holualoa church where Norman Sakata was scoutmaster for Post 26. Having grown up in Holualoa, the son of a Japanese immigrant laborer, and a young *nisei* woman, Scoutmaster Sakata was a family man, an active member of the Holualoa community, and had been a coffee farmer, a truck driver and a successful surplus supply businessman. A member of a large family (he had ten brothers and sisters, one of whom earned distinction as the wrestler and actor "Oddjob" Sakata), Sakata remembered the poverty and lack of opportunity of his youth. Following service in the United States Army with the 39th Infantry Battalion, he returned to Holualoa determined to improve himself. He prepared himself to successfully pass the exams for a high school diploma and entered scouting in 1954 as a means to help the young people of the community. By the time Ellison asked Mr. Sakata for permission to enter scouting, Post 26 had become one of the finest, most active and youth-building scouting units in the islands.

Masamitsu Onizuka took special pride in the achievements of his children. Ellison dines with his Dad, September 1960. (Onizuka Family)

45

A Brother Remembers

*Claude Onizuka recalled his memory of his brother at his home in Kona
on a stormy Sunday afternoon. He possesses a quiet humor that immediately puts
someone at ease. His words are measured as he candidly remembered
the years of his youth and his love for his brother.*

❝ *I think I like to picture Ellison with the space program.
He was very satisfied with what he had accomplished and was
really looking forward to returning after the second flight. He could share
more things with the people. I think of him coming out of the crew port
smiling and waving, with the space program. Whatever we do we have to
preserve his memory. Besides his family, the space program was his life.
There is no doubt in my mind he'd want us to do everything we could to
support the program. NASA is going through rough times and
we should stand behind it. It was something he worked to achieve
and we should support it to go on.* **❞**

*OPPOSITE: In the basement of this old
Holualoa Church, Ellison one night in 1960
joined Explorer Post 26. ABOVE: The
4-H Club was an important part of
Ellison's upbringing.*

Scoutmaster Sakata and his younger volunteer assistant adviser, Matthew Heneralau, watched Ellison Onizuka grow up in scouting. The Boy Scouts seemed tailor made for Ellison—it demanded his energy, his commitment, and his desire for perfection and attainment. In turn it gave him a recognition and honor he seemed very much to need and a fulfillment of involvement with his personal and public life. "He was a smart boy," Sakata recalls of his very first impression, "intelligent and well-mannered." This boy stood out, he explains, although not necessarily because he was "better" or "more outstanding" than the other youths. What impressed the Scoutmaster was that Ellison was determined, took responsibility and most importantly showed respect for his elders, his parents and his roots. He was one of the few scouts to be re-elected to the presidency of the organization—the members voted their own leadership.

ABOVE: The Konawaena High School paper, the Wildcat, announces the election of Ellison Onizuka as Class Treasurer, July 3, 1963. RIGHT: Keopu Cemetery sign, erected as a community project by Post 26.

Ellison had not been either a cub scout or a boy scout so that when he joined the program at the age of fourteen, he entered the explorers, a category designed for older boys. Consequently, Elllison was one of the first scouts to attain the highest rank of eagle through a special path just being set up for this special group of older scouts. To earn the rank, he had to demonstrate outstanding achievement in a number of areas: vocational skills, community service, social development, citizenship advancement and outdoor life. Ellison's commitment to community service was especially important. Mr. Sakata had always emphasized community service—the boys put up signs at the Holualoa cemetery, for example, one year. They used to pick coffee beans so as to raise enough money to donate a koa wood mobile bookrack to the Kona Hospital. They helped poison weeds, they renovated the basement of the deserted Holualoa Church which now served as their meeting hall, and they would do a "litter clean up" of Captain Cook's Monument at Kealakekua Bay. The old spirit of *kumiai* was very much alive in Post 26.

In the fulfillment of his eagle rank, Ellison attained excellence in all achievement areas. "Everything he did," Matthew Heneralau now recalls, "he became number one man." For service achievement he beautified his Buddhist temple in Keopu. He helped prevent erosion in the area by personally making a drainage ditch to keep the soil and planted grass in the area. His merit badges, which he proudly wore on a sash draped across his chest, reveal his successes at outdoor life and camping. To earn his citizenship merit badge, he helped to write the by-laws of his explorer post. The document, which Scoutmaster Sakata preserved over the years, is a carefully constructed constitution with an interesting clause revealing the young man's solid upbringing and sense of family respect. In his listing of the organization's objectives, Ellison included the usual exhortations promoting good citizenship, physical fitness, leadership, moral character, service to community and curbing delinquency. But he also noted that the object of the explorers was to "stimulate independency to alleviate the burden of parents." He could be a well-behaved *mohan seinen*.

Scouting also gave to the adolescent Ellison a wider scope of social activities. For most teenagers, the hangouts in Kona had been relatively simple. When, for example, Ellison and his high school friends and baseball teammates Stan Oka or Earl Ogata got together, they'd go to the only bowling alley in all of Kona, in Kainaliu. The alley closed after a couple years although the sign remains, as does the memory of hearing pins strike at all hours on the street outside. Or they ate at nearby Teshima's which had Japanese or American local style food. Parties were at friends' houses and when they later came of age, they enjoyed their beer. For movies, there was the Aloha Theatre, which mixed American, Japanese and Filipino films during the week to meet all sorts of tastes. Not too many of the guys had cars—Ellison was lucky because his father used to let him use the family car a lot. They sometimes got into the mainland fads and they listened to Elvis, Pat Boone and the Beatles, but all that seemed pretty remote to the Kona gang. They played pranks, though Ellison was, as Stan Oka observes, "pretty smart. He never got caught." Probably the most memorable prank was pulled by a visiting Honolulu high school baseball player who once, when riding in Ellison's jeep, pulled his pants down and mooned the main Kona drag.

The official scouting social dances and visits from girl scouts from the neighbor islands were a big deal for the explorers. It was their opportunity to test their charm and dating skills on a fresh batch of young ladies. Twisting was still popular, as was the bunny hop. And in one old black-and-white photograph, Ellison is captured groomed in his scout uniform, clinging to a young lady's hip as the bunny hop train winds its way through the memory of those innocent adolescent days. Although he was not aggressive when it came

An explorer scout badge Ellison saved from his Kona boyhood.

49

Ellison's eagle rank medal and his achievement cards—the tributes from attaining the Boy Scouts' highest honor.

to dating the opposite sex, neither was Ellison backwards. He did his share of socializing and scouting gave him an excellent sense of confidence.

He also learned to push himself to the limit of physical endurance. President Kennedy was actively inspiring the young people in those days to go beyond the limit, to get tough and be prepared, to ask what they could do for their country and to become physically fit. The challenge went out across the country to young people to participate in a fifty mile hike as a symbol of American youth and strength. In response, Post 26 took the challenge. However, since Scoutmaster Sakata was a Republican, he suggested to the boys that they do the President one better—that they hike fifty-one miles. So one cool evening the parents drove the troop up to Mt. Kohala above Waimea and most of them made the long trek back to Holualoa. For months they had trained for the walk, preparing themselves for the challenge and daring to go further. Ellison and Claude both finished the fifty-one mile hike.

Because of their public service activities and fundraisers, Ellison's scouting unit was relatively wealthy and could afford holding family affairs and ceremonies honoring those youths who had attained eagle rank, or for their graduating school class. Thus, Ellison was exposed to the ceremonial dinner which later would become an all too regular feature of his public life. His greatest moment was no doubt the ceremony in which he was honored for his attainment of the eagle rank. Three other explorers had earned the merit together, so, in a memorable banquet at the old King Kamehameha Hotel in Kailua, Ellison and his friends were feted by peers, family and friends. His mother notes his love for uniforms—she remembers how he always wanted his scouting or baseball uniforms to be immaculate and clean. That night a proud Ellison Onizuka, in his fresh, pressed uniform, took his first bite of manhood and enjoyed it fully. It was an appetite for achievement he never lost.

He also never lost the comfort he felt when speaking before large crowds. Scoutmaster Sakata had helped to instill in his boys a confidence to step up in front of large groups and express oneself. Every boy in the scouts took some turn at a leadership role and was encouraged in public speaking. In fact, if they were late to a meeting, they were required to give a short speech explaining their tardiness—an interesting scheme that made Claude turn around and go home rather than be late if he saw Mr. Sakata's car parked in front of the church. Ellison was a confident, well-paced public speaker who entered speech contests at high school and was often called upon to address large crowds. Although among his friends he could speak pidgin English with finesse, when needed, his standard English was resonate, measured and without flaw. As president of the explorers, he enjoyed leading meetings, demonstrating a startling precise command of Robert's Rules of Order without having to look up the text. Many of his high school classmates say that although they can not remember the content of the speeches, they can vividly recall the affect on the audience. When he spoke, fellow 4-H'er Susan Morimoto explains, "he had a quiet but charismatic manner. He was shy but could appear very confident of which direction he wanted to go. That's why his speeches always got him elected."

Matthew Heneralau can still describe the rousing impact of a speech Ellison presented one night to the Rotary Club. They had given the explorer post an honorary dinner and, as president, Ellison was required to make a small address. Matthew remembers clearly the final line which was met with enthusiastic applause: "American ends with two words: I Can." Scouting had taught the young boy a patriotism and pride of confidence that he was to retain for the remainder of his life.

All the various traits—the ambition, the enjoyment of recognition, the sacrifice to community, the confidence of self-presentation, the speaking, learning and writing skills, the hard work and determination as well as the stubbornness and temper—added up by the end of high school to forge the Ellison Onizuka that was to leave Kona with a dream of the stars. For the dream to become a reality, he would have to face perhaps his greatest obstacle—the powerful, sobering and conservative effects of adulthood.

ABOVE: The merit badge sash Ellison proudly wore as an Explorer. LEFT: Masamitsu Onizuka escorts two visiting Shinto priests around Kona in the mid-1950s. (Onizuka Family) OVERLEAF: Sunset on the earth as thunder clouds cast their long shadows into the dusk. Photographed from Skylab orbiter, 1973. (NASA)

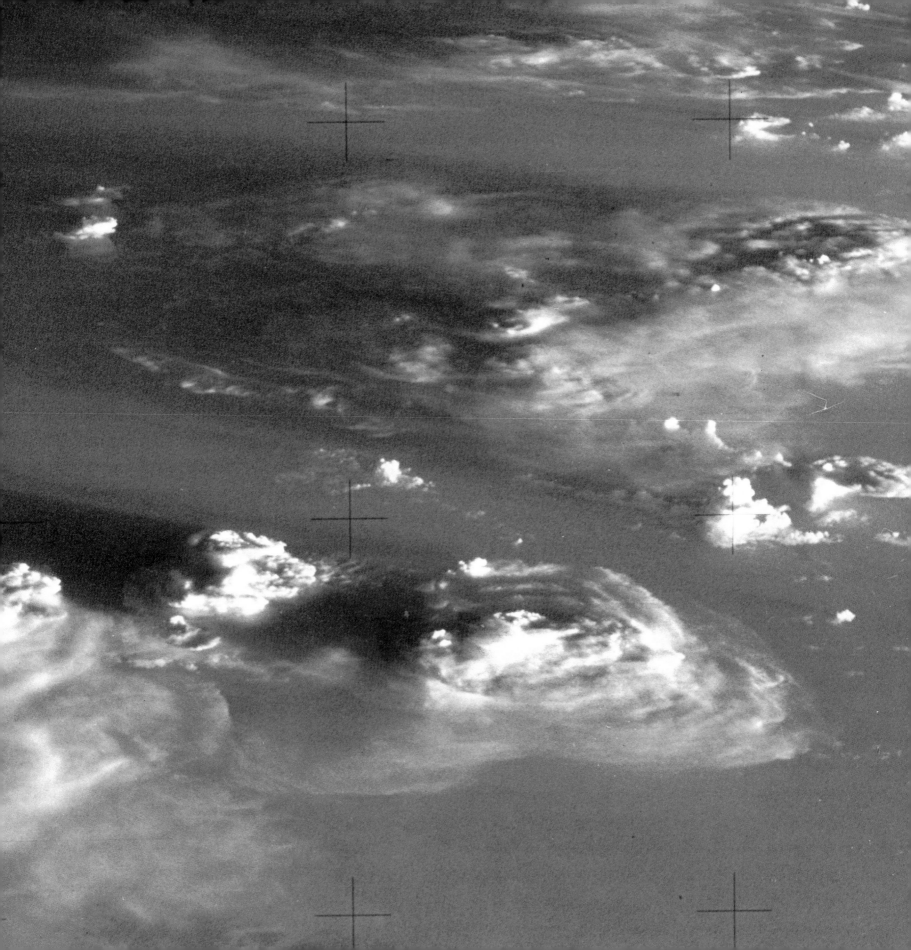

CHAPTER FOUR

"Wind Enkindles the Great"

University of Colorado freshman Onizuka poses in his ROTC uniform at Boulder, Colorado, in December, 1964.
(Onizuka Family)

At the age of eighteen Ellison must have felt that he was sitting on top of the world. He was graduating from Konawaena High School with top honors, was on a champion baseball team and was highly respected by his classmates. The scouts in his explorer post had twice elected him to the office of president. He was also a statewide president of the 4-H Club, as well as of the Young Buddhist Association. He had a gang of friends he loved, girl friends to date and a family to support him. Although he was not accepted for college by the Air Force Academy, his first selection, he was honored to be admitted by the University of Colorado as a freshman in their Fall 1964 semester. Mr. Sakata had written a letter of recommendation for him to the Standard Oil Company in favor of a 4-H educational scholarship. He was awarded three hundred dollars to help defray expenses. If anyone was braced for success in adulthood, it was Ellison Onizuka.

When the Class of '64 received their sheepskins, they were formally entering an adult world that was, unknown to most of them, becoming fraught with unrest and danger. But as far as they were concerned, the Vietnam War was an ugly police action in a far away Asian land, and student unrest was limited to the "beatniks" of Berkeley. Drugs had not gotten out of hand, hair was still relatively short and the "generation gap" had not quite yet been invented. In the new State of Hawaii, in the high country of Kona, the brewing storms of unrest must have seemed even further distant and unreal. Life after high school still meant, for the Kona Class of '64, college, settling down, marriage, career, children and a mortgage. Under the yearbook photographs each graduate received a "quotation of life" to navigate them into adulthood. For Ellison Onizuka the selected quote was prophetic: "Wind Enkindles the Great."

Embarking on adulthood meant for many Kona youths a drastic separation from family. Ironically, in this close-knit rural community, where family and neighbors were the fabric of one's life, the children were expected to go to college on the mainland. Coffee farmers who struggled to keep their families secure in the often insecure agricultural business, still set aside their savings so that their children could get an excellent education on the mainland. Counselors at Konawaena High School began advising college-bound students on careers, curriculums and universities that might meet their needs. Applications for admission were sent out and the word of confirmation or rejection was waited for with great peer group anticipation. While no firm figures exist on how many Kona graduates left for mainland colleges, Norman

Ellison doing knee bends in the living room of his Keopu home. (Onizuka Family)

Sakata noted that over half of the explorers in his post would go away to college. So Ellison was not alone in his determination to go to the University of Colorado in Boulder. His parents approved of and supported the decision, while his friends were also going away to mainland colleges.

However, unlike the majority of graduates who were going into education, business, law, pre-med or agriculture, Ellison announced that he was going to study aerospace engineering. Both the Air Force Academy and the University of Colorado had excellent programs in the field. Some of his friends were surprised and puzzled by the decision—what kind of engineering was that and did it make good money? Ellison always made up his own mind. He liked to do things in his own way—like the time he jumped out of Stan Oka's car and challenged to race the vehicle down Mamalahoa Highway on foot! He lost the race, but he won the respect of his peers, in that he was not to be persuaded by the pressure of others.

At home, his mother and father accepted his career decision without question. "We left it up to him," his mother now reflects. "Be what you want to be, study hard and don't be a dropout," he was told. A working class family where the father drives a taxi and works a coffee field and the mother tends a store doesn't often provide much educational stimulation. Mrs. Onizuka used to help Ellison with his homework by timing how fast he would write his essays. He liked to set time limits for himself and see if he could break them. Other than that, his parents had no time to see what kinds of books he was reading or follow what he was learning. All they could hope for was that through their labors and his success in school, he would inherit a priceless gift of education. "We can't give you property or money," his mother remembers telling Ellison. "Education is all we have to give you. Nobody can take that away from you. It's all for you."

As traditional and close as the Onizuka family was, there was a marvelous spirit of freedom given to the children as they reached adulthood. As Shirley observes, "our family always tried to give us what we wanted. 'Be sure to ask', we were told, and if they could they would get it. They never deprived us of anything." When Norma went away to Honolulu to go to business college, for example, her father would always send her money to come home for a weekend. The family should stay close, he believed, even if the children went away for their education and later marriage. Nurtured in this type of parental support, left free to choose his own destiny as long as it brought honor, Ellison did not have to endure many of the conflicts or turmoils that often marked the maturation of others of his generation.

The most difficult passage of maturity he had to face was the isolation and separation of his first years at college. Kona had not only been comforting and secure, but a world where achievements were rewarded with applause and respect. He was never a glory hound. He never sought achievement solely for honor or fame. As Norman Sakata remembers, when someone held up a camera to take a picture, he never joined the other boys who leaped in to have their photograph taken. That was not like Ellison. But the accolades were there—the love and support always evident. In Colorado he was a stranger and at first a loner. He was on his own, free to make his own decisions in an unfamiliar world and he yearned for his active, ambitious Kona life.

Ellison wrote several letters to his former scoutmaster during his first year at the University of Colorado. Not only do the letters reveal his strong sense of values, but they indicate that Ellison was beginning to take what novelist Sherwood Anderson would call the "backward view of life." No longer a boy doing his chores and shooting baskets, no longer one of two dozen scouts going on hikes or cleaning up Kona cemeteries, he saw himself as a man who could look back to his youth and offer advice. His first letter, written on September 25, 1964 at Boulder, Colorado, thanked Mr. Sakata and Matthew Heneralau for their four years of assistance and support. "Exploring is really a fine way to make a person confident of himself," he wrote, expressing his hope that "all of

In the early 1960's, Kona teen-agers would gather at the second-floor bowling alley in Kainaliu. Although the alley has been long closed and the pins are no longer heard crashing from the streets below, the sign remains of the former "hang out."

Ellison takes a playful break in studying at his University of Colorado apartment, 1969. OPPOSITE TOP: The Kona boy masters a strange new vehicle—skis, at Winter Park, Colorado, in December 1965. OPPOSITE BOTTOM: College "hi-jinks" at the University of Colorado. (Onizuka Family)

The Embarrassed Hero

Ellison Onizuka received much fame in his lifetime. But his former Scoutmaster, Norman Sakata, recalls how ill-at-ease the astronaut felt when given too much attention. Interviewed in his Holualoa home, Scoutmaster Sakata leafs through the album of mementoes he has saved over the years of the boys who had been part of explorer Post 26. Ellison obviously stands out in his memory as a young man who achieved much but retained a firm, humble grasp on his roots. He did not seek the limelight, as Norman Sakata remembers, for selfish reasons.

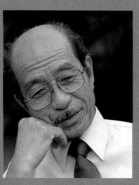  

After Ellison was first selected to become an astronaut for NASA, in my mind he was the same old Ellison. "Mr. Sakata," he would still say. He never changed in my mind. Never significantly. He was still very humble. He took the fame bashfully. It was embarrassing for him. When the Prince of Japan came last year for the 100th anniversary of Japanese immigration, the Kona Japanese Civic Association hosted the program. As the master of ceremony, I saw Ellison's name listed on the head table. The Mayor of Hawaii had requested Ellison to be at the head table. I asked if Ellison knew. "No," I was told by the planners, "it was going to be a surprise." I knew it would embarrass him. I told him, and he said, "No, I'm not going up there. This isn't my night." That's the kind of man he was. The limelight came for his accomplishments, but he didn't do it for the limelight. He was embarrassed he got so much attention. That's how I size him up.

the boys will take exploring seriously. The social and developmental aspects of scouting are surely helping me." Even at eighteen he could see that his childhood had ended, the "fundamentals that I got as a scout" had made him a man and "a well-rounded citizen."

In a separate letter written to the explorers of Post 26, Ellison offered the observation that "everything that I have within me today would not have been possible without the guidance of Mr. Sakata and Matthew, and your cooperation in letting me practice them. All the discipline and guidance that were acquired on my journey to the Castle of Eagles are a major part of my priceless treasure chest today." He goes on to offer a wonderfully uplifting, sagacious bit of advice to scouts he now sees as "juniors" in his past:

"As a member of the Air Force ROTC, I find that all the training that I got as a scout in marching, discipline, care of a uniform, esprit de corps, and initiative imbued confidence and the drive to be a top notch officer in the 105th Cadet Corps into me. In Post 26, Mr. Sakata, and Matthew, you have the best advisorship that can be found anywhere. Mr. Sakata and Matthew are dedicated individuals, whom any organization would welcome with open arms. They will never fail you; give them your fullest cooperation and be sincere to them, for you are lucky to have them. They are the ones who have watched over the colors of Post 26 for a long time, they have deviated its activities from failure quite often, and it is through them that Post 26 is what it is today. They are responsible for your actions so remember them in all that you do. The prestige and pride of "Post 26" should always be considered in your undertakings…Carry out the functions of Post 26 in the true manner that it has always been done. Best wishes and Good Luck to all of you for another year of glory and success for Post 26 and its activities."

In addition to assuming a new role with the explorers as one of the "older generation," Ellison also revealed a homesickness and loneliness in his letter. To Mr. Sakata he wrote that "now that I am all alone by myself, I find that everything is strange in adult life. I am alone to make all of my own decisions and carry on my expectations." He wanted to know how things were in "good old Kona" and though he was thousands of miles away, he offered that "if I may be of assistance to you or the Post, please feel free to call on me." Before he left, he had been given a "farewell banquet," which a month later was "still vividly recalled." Three months later he typed up a New Year's greetings letter to the Post in which he surmised their present activities, and called them onward to further accomplishments. He had been following their progress, he admitted, in letters from his family. "In whatever you do," he admonished them, "remember to 'stand tall, walk tall, and most of all, think tall.'" In a postscript to Mr. Sakata, he wrote "Boulder, Colo. is an awfully nice place and it's quite cold here. If you have the time, visit this state." The Kona boy was cold, lonely and homesick.

As he noted in his letter, his love and respect for scouting were continued in his membership in the Air Force ROTC which he joined as a University of

Ellison continued to earn honors in college for outstanding achievement in the Air Force ROTC. (Onizuka Family)

Colorado freshman. Perhaps the loneliness of living away from Hawaii was compensated through his involvement in the Air Force. Ellison never balked at the discipline of the military life. He was a patriot who loved his country, felt proud when saluting his flag and wore his uniform with distinction. While campuses across the nation were, by the late 1960's, erupting in anti-war violence and demonstrations, the Colorado campus was relatively quiet. As an ROTC cadet, Ellison was exempt from the active military draft, plus he had a loyalty to his superiors. Most importantly, his brother Claude, who had joined the Hawaii National Guard so as to be a weekend soldier, had been activated and sent to Vietnam. It was unlikely that Ellison, devoted to his country and family, would have felt anything but support for the policies of the government.

He threw himself into his studies, especially enjoying the challenge of working in a team. One special project was designing and constructing a model weather observation airplane, which several schoolmates and he made for a class assignment. He was animated, involved and hardworking when the challenge of such a project was put before him. Even in his studies, the prospects of the social unit working together for a common goal brought out the very best in Ellison. He developed a close friendship with his roommate Norman Sato, learned to get along with all kinds of University of Colorado students, and knew how to put his studies aside to socialize on Friday nights and weekends. Within a year he was following a familiar pattern—leader of his cadets, well-known and liked around campus, and active in a variety of college organizations, including one composed of a small group of Hawaii-born students. He spent summers at home in Kona (his father liked to keep the family together). Winter vacations were spent skiing in the Rockies. Ellison had discovered a whole new mainland experience, though he retained the informal, friendly style of a "local boy."

Love also entered his adult life. Ellison's college roommate, Norman Sato, was dating Estelle Jimbo of Hilo, who was attending the University of Northern Colorado in nearby Greeley. When Norman used to go up to visit Estelle, Ellison would sometimes tag along. There he met Estelle's friend and fellow University of Northern Colorado classmate, Lorna Leiko Yoshida. He and Lorna started joining the same partying groups and Estelle began to do some old-fashioned matchmaking. Figuring that it was easier to play along with Estelle than fight it, they pretended to go out together even though they were dating other people—then it got real. On Thanksgiving Day, 1967, they went out on their first date to a dinner given by friends for Hawaii students. They were an "item" after that, Ellison visiting Greeley whenever possible.

My training is continuing at a pretty good pace and the technical projects, speaking assignments and other jobs keep us pretty busy. I've been assigned to work on NASA's Solid Spinning Upper Stage (SSUS) as a technical assignment. In addition, I've given a few short tours of the Johnson Space Center to some of the distinguished visitors to NASA JSC and a bunch of interviews for newspapers and TV/Radio. In the past months I've talked to quite a few of the press from Japan. My speech in Seattle went over very well and got good coverage in the area. Hopefully, it helped the people there and did some good for NASA.

Lorna was the daughter of Herbert and Anna Yoshida, who resided in Naalehu at the far south district of Ka'u on Hawaii. Her father worked for Hutchinson Sugar in Ka'u and her mother was a "multi-purpose" person for the Naalehu Elementary School. During the school year she worked in the cafetorium and during summers in the library. Lorna's paternal grandparents had immigrated from the prefecture of Niigata in Japan and had been plantation laborers in the Ka'u area. Like Ellison, Lorna had grown up a third generation *sansei* country girl in a close-knit community. Her life was busy with school, church and the array of social clubs and organizations that made a rural teenage existence in the sixties quite busy. In fact, Lorna had been a chapter president of the Young Buddhist Association at a time when Ellison was also a member. That was when she first became aware of her future husband, although they never dated or showed an interest in one another. Ellison was three years older, and in high school that was a considerable age span. She was also in 4-H, and when reports would go up the organizational ladder to the state level, they would come back approved by the state president, Ellison Onizuka.

Anxious to taste life beyond the tiny remote community of Naalehu, Lorna had applied to Colorado State College (CSC), which later became the University of Northern Colorado. Colorado was attracting a lot of Hawaii

LEFT: Living on the mainland as an Air Force officer, Ellison always tried to keep in close contact with his Kona family. In this letter to his mother following his selection to NASA in 1978, he shares with her, his new responsibilities and accomplishments. ABOVE: An ROTC honor awarded to Ellison at the University of Colorado.

61

ABOVE: *Lorna and Ellison pose in "jail" at Abilene, Texas during their courtship. RIGHT: Quiet moments on Hapuna Beach, Hawaii, would later become Lorna's and Ellison's favorite retreat from the hectic routine of an astronaut's life.*

students and the Naalehu Community Club offered her a scholarship to help pay her way. With the encouragement of her parents, she left for college in the fall of 1967. Self-confident, on her own, not afraid to express herself and socially active, she majored in special education with a minor in psychology. When she again met the Kona boy with the winning smile in Colorado, she was far from impressed. "I had a false stereotype of what El was," she now recalls. "Because he was president of this and that, I expected him to be socially absent. When I met him at college, I still had that image of him." Afterall, he had continued his high school reputation in college—president of his student association, a pacesetter, and all the leadership roles. "As far as I was concerned," says Lorna, "I had assumed that El would have to be a social 'nerd'."

But after they started dating, she discovered that El was no "egghead"—he had a sense of humor, an ease with friends and could be great fun at parties. He loved playing tricks on people and knew how to ease off and, in "local style," lay back. He had the academic and leadership images, but Lorna fell in love with the informal, fun-loving young man who was able to earn the respect and friendship of people he met with his good humor. In turn, here was a woman who could join him in his peer group socializing—who was as anxious as he was to enjoy friends on Friday night beer busts or weekend group activities. She was articulate, involved in campus life and also knew how to laugh. They made good companions and in her own way, Lorna brought a certain down-to-earth edge of responsibility to the young man who could become at times over-involved and over-giving to his friends.

In the last few months of his senior year, in February of 1968, Ellison returned from an ROTC meeting to receive a telephone call from his sister in Keopu that nearly ended his dream of becoming an aerospace engineer. Masamitsu had just finished working in the coffee field when he suddenly had a fatal heart attack. Ellison flew home to Kona. He knew, as the oldest son, the responsibility for the store, the coffee lands and his mother would now fall to him. All of his boyhood dreams of becoming an aerospace engineer would now have to be displaced as the needs of his family came first. When he arrived in Keopu for his father's funeral he also realized what at a distance was hard to grasp—his father was gone.

Young Ellison and his father had been very close. In many ways, they had resembled one another. Masamitsu was known for his friendliness, his out-going manner and his community involvement. He belonged to church organizations, an athletic booster club and even helped out when Ellison and Claude were in the scouts. He was a scout committeeman and helped Norman Sakata with community activities and especially transportation. The night that the boys were driven to Mt. Kohala for their fifty-one mile trek, it was Masamitsu with other fathers that transported them up the mountain and then proudly followed them down in case a boy needed a ride. He enjoyed driving the boys all around the island and when he could, joined them at the beach. As Claude recalls, "he wasn't too strict with us. He'd get mad, but he wasn't *strict*-strict." He encouraged the boys to get their driver's licenses when they were young and allowed them liberal use of the family car, even when they brought it home with cracked rear end's or burnt bearings. But he kept a watchful eye. On the wall of the garage he penciled in the mileage on the odometer before and after they used the car. "Where did you go," he'd ask one of them periodically if the mileage was excessive for a young teenager just driving around Captain Cook.

Proud of what Ellison was becoming, the father had sacrificed much to give his oldest son the best education possible. So when the grieving son suggested to his mother that he might drop out of college and take care of business in Keopu, she strongly told him to go back and finish his semester. By any measure, Mitsue Onizuka would be adjudged strong. Her manner is so charmingly quiet and gentle, her mind sharp and yet tinged with an "old country" deference that perhaps it would seem unreasonable to suppose to give her the burden of too much responsibility. But for nearly a quarter of a century she had run the little store in front of the house and had helped to hold her family together. Now with Masamitsu gone, the responsibilities would become

Ellison receives his ROTC medal. (Onizuka Family)

ABOVE: *Honorary certification awarded to Ellison for outstanding scholarship by Tau Beta Pi association of the University of Colorado.*
OPPOSITE: *The Tau Beta Pi medallion.*

even greater, but she responded without self-pity or complaint. She would do what she had to do so that her son could have the tools to make something of himself.

Ellison spent ten days in Keopu following his father's funeral, assured his mother that he would do whatever was necessary to help her, and then returned to his final semester of study. He began a regular practice of calling his mother, to check on her progress and that of the store. Even though Claude and Shirley lived nearby, it was the oldest son who lived on the mainland that she relied upon. At one point the phone calls were becoming so expensive that she told Ellison to write letters, as it was less costly. In turn he told her what to stock in the store, suggesting that she only handle the well-known brand name products. "Don't listen to salesmen who want you to stock the new things," he said. "People in Keopu will always go for the tried and true."

Buddhism also offered strength to Ellison. He had been brought up a devout Honpa Hongwanji Buddhist and had attended regular services at the little picturesque Hongwanji temple in Keopu that he had helped to beautify as an explorer. On the weekends he had attended Japanese language school— they had no *sensei* during the week since Keopu was so small. With such infrequent lessons, the young *sansei* never became proficient at Japanese, though he could understand a little and speak a few phrases. As children, the family encouraged traditional celebrations at New Years, and during the summer the young boys would don *hapi* coats and join the Bon dancing. If anything marked young Ellison as an ethnic Japanese, it was his love for the food of the homeland. Although his favorite dinner was steak—"Hmmm, that's a meal, Mom"—he loved the pungent, sticky *natto* fermented bean which Grandmother Onizuka would prepare.

Before going to college, his parents had advised him that if he felt that it was necessary for him to become a Christian so as to adjust in Colorado, then he should do so. Later, when he came home, he could become a Buddhist again. In the remarkable tolerance of their faith, the Onizukas felt that Ellison's social adjustment on the mainland was far more important than singling himself out as religiously different. But he evidently did not take their advice. After all, this was the boy who, when he lost his gold Buddhist emblem that he wore around his neck, frantically insisted to his father that they should screen the sand at Kahaluu Beach where the emblem had been lost. When it wasn't found, the father purchased him a new one which he was to wear for the rest of his life. It was unlikely that he could doff his religion for Christianity as easily as taking off a hat.

At the 100th day memorial service for his father, he drove into Denver and visited the Tri-State Buddhist Church. He sat alone in the sanctuary, the Hawaii-born *sansei* who believed firmly in the sacredness of life, and prayed his

"He also inspired me."

At a Kona seaside restaurant on a Saturday afternoon, several high school classmates of Ellison Onizuka joined a group interview. Earl Ogata, Caroline Nakashima, Susan Morimoto, Lynn Bradley, Nathan Kurashige and Stan Oka shared their nostalgia for "small kid time" and the years they spent together in those adolescent years. At the end of the session, Stan Oka perhaps expressed a common sentiment most eloquently.

" *The last time Ellison came home, after his first flight, I had a chance to talk to him. He came to the high school and he had about an hour before he had to go to the auditorium. So we sat down together in this small lounge and we were just talking. We had gone through the same thing together. Even when he was in high school I looked at him as someone who had a plan. He didn't say, "This is what I want to be," but I think he knew exactly what he was going to be. Someone asked me if he was a dreamer. And I answered I don't think he was a dreamer, but he was someone who planned ahead. As I talked to Ellison and I looked at him, I wondered how he got this far when we all started at the same place. I wasn't jealous but I was just thinking about how he did it. And as he went out to talk to the kids he was trying to show the things that he did—how he had made his dreams come true. If you want to do it also, he told the children, you can do it. He inspired a lot of kids. But he also inspired me. He was a friend but I looked at him in a different light. I talked to his sister and I told her that. I look at Ellison and I think about Ellison. I think of the loss of what he could have done because of the type of person he was. That's the impression I have left of him.* **"**

sutras for the spirit of his father, that he might cross the bridge of life and death and find eternal peace in the Pureland. Never before must he have felt more alone or more determined to strive to honor the memory of his father.

Graduation from the University of Colorado a few months later might have been a bit more sober in the wake of his father's death, but his mother still flew to the ceremonies marking her son's triumphal passage into full adulthood. His plans were to go into an accelerated Master of Science program in aerospace engineering and then enter the Air Force. It seemed that in Ellison's life, honors and celebrations always rushed in on each other. The "winds" which enkindled greatness also blew strong and steady for this young man. On the same day that Ellison graduated, he was commissioned a second lieutenant and his mother proudly pinned the bars on his uniform. The next day, June 7, 1969, Lorna and he were married at the Tri-State Buddhist Church in Denver. Ellison's mother and aunt, Mrs. Tomeyo Nagata, were joined by Lorna's mother, father and maternal grandmother, Mrs. Yamamoto, who flew to Colorado for the marriage ceremony and reception, which included a large number of students, friends, professors and staff. Although she still had a few years to go before finishing college, she deferred her own education for marriage and Ellison's career. By December of 1969 he had received his Master of Science degree in aerospace engineering, and he entered active duty with the United States Air Force in January 1970, after receiving his commission at the University of Colorado through the four-year ROTC program as a distinguished military graduate. He was a member of Tau Beta Pi, Sigma Tau and Triangle Fraternity.

As close as they were to one another, her new Air Force husband never shared with Lorna any interest in space travel. He did have, she observed, a strong sense of direction in the way he mapped out his assignments and jobs. After finishing school, his first assignment was to McClellan Air Force Base in Sacramento, California, where he received his First Lieutenant rank. From there he pursued a career that took him to the top of his ranking as a flight test engineer. "Everything he did," Lorna confides, "he was never unsure. I think he knew what blocks he needed to fill and preplanned his dream." She thinks now that if he had told her about his desire to fly to the stars, he would have thought she would not really understand. "And he was probably right." Only a few times did he ever talk about space travel, and then only lightly. Once she remembers him joking after hearing some news report about the successful landing of a manned flight to the moon, "I'm going to take a shot at that." The Kona Air Force officer had an uncanny aim.

OPPOSITE: *Second Lieutenant Ellison S. Onizuka and his bride Lorna, on their wedding day, June 7, 1969.* ABOVE: *The newlyweds cut their wedding cake at their reception in Colorado, June 7, 1969. (Onizuka Family)* OVERLEAF: *The effects of living in space for prolonged periods of time is explored on Skylab, an orbiting experimental laboratory. Three crews inhabited the orbiter for nearly six months in 1973 and 1974. (NASA)*

67

CHAPTER FIVE
Ellison S. Onizuka, Flight Test Engineer

The excitement of the early U.S. manned space flights captured the national interest in the 1960's. In an historic rendezvous of two Gemini earth orbiters, Gemini 7 is photographed miles above the earth from Gemini 6 in December, 1965. (NASA)

I t was a boyhood ambition, he had told his mother, to become an engineer—any kind of engineer just as long as engineer was tagged on to the end of his name. He had told a reporter years later how, in 1959, he had witnessed the eruption of Kilauea Iki crater with half a dozen of his schoolmates from Honokohau Elementary School. While the other kids were oogle-eyed over the beauty and fiery brilliance of the 1,500 ft. fountain of molten lava, young Ellison was preoccupied with the problem of how all that energy could be controlled. Even as a thirteen-year-old adolescent, he confessed, he had the mind of an engineer.

When a man flies to the stars, we sometimes falsely assume that his life up to that point must have resembled a Buck Rogers romance of daring and high flying adventure. We forget that much of life is as mundane and ordinary for the star voyager as it is for us. The years in the Air Force were for Ellison a time of training, preparation and long hours in a regular work schedule. At McClellan Air Force Base he participated in flight test programs and systems safety engineering for a great variety of aircraft including the F-84, F-100, F-105, F-111, EC-121T, T-33, T-39, T-28 and A-1. The work entailed lots of research and design time, long office hours and frustrations. "Work is alright," he wrote his mother in October of 1970, "but it's a drag at times. Many times I wish that it could be a little better with good results. The reason I said that was because we had to throw away nine months work since we had made a small mistake when the project was started." He often rationalized such delays over tiny details with a philosophical acceptance. "Well, I guess everything has to be perfect," he explained to his mother, "and I know it so it doesn't bother me that much."

Life in Sacramento was, as he often complained in letters to his mother, chilly and damp. Lorna was attempting to continue her education at night while their infant daughter Janelle was going through her growing pains. Ellison helped out as much as he could, watching Janelle, taking her for walks in the park, which she adored, and trying to make ends meet with car insurance, household expenses and Lorna's schooling. "Don't get the impression that we're broke," he once wrote his mother when he delayed paying her a small debt. "We're managing alright and whatever isn't used is being saved for later."

Parenthood was a new and challenging experience for both Lorna and Ellison. And it was not without its moments of difficulty. The first time they had to sterilize baby bottle nipples they realized how unprepared they were for "bringing up baby." Ellison had purchased a dozen nipples and explained to Lorna that she had better sterilize them in boiling water. Using a new pot, Lorna put the rubber nipples in boiling water which she soon left unattended.

Test flight engineer Onizuka climbs aboard a F-105 jet fighter at McClellan Air Force Base, Sacramento, California, 1972.

A Gift for the Yonsei

Lorna Onizuka is a poised, articulate young woman who shared with her husband love for Hawaii and a commitment to the community. She has a wonderful and warm sense of humor that immediately puts one at ease. Her interview at the home of Claude Onizuka provided candid insights into her husband, her family, marriage and the years as the wife of an astronaut.

" *I watched Ellison get raptured when he talked with other people about space travel. When I asked him what it was really like, he said he could never share that with anybody. It was so much better than anything he had ever done. It was very eery to listen to him talk about it. He could not find words for his feelings. The quiet hours afterward, he was not bubbling like he was before the flight. He was at peace, quiet. The first night after he got down, I asked him about how he felt, but I was disturbing something important and too private. Slowly I saw him build back up to describe some of his feelings. None of the astronauts can tell you what it is really like. You won't know unless you go yourself. Ellison waited so long and it meant so much to him. He used simple words, like "it was the best, the most fantastic," but his face was bursting. What Ellison felt is something I have never experienced and never will. But I was not jealous.*

He felt an obligation to share that special experience with the children. Not an obligation like a debt—but an obligation of return for everything he had. That was always prominent. It was like a sharing back with the community. I used to think, "Why did he fill up his schedule so tight?" It was important to him to do it. When El came back home it was not for the pomp and fanfare. He would cram in ninety post-flight appearances. He had energy to do it. He was tired, but he kept going. It was the only way he could say thank you. That seemed real important to him.

I hope that the children will remember how much doing what he did was what he wanted to do. How much he tried to let them know there is no impossible dream. The enthusiasm he had for the need for exploration was his gift. Not the long hours, they were important to me. Not to him.

Ellison S. Onizuka, bowler. (Onizuka Family)

An hour later, when Ellison came home, he asked Lorna if he could taste the corn chowder cooking on the range. When she replied that she did not know what he was talking about, they discovered that the water had evaporated and the nipples were a mass of melted rubber. When the conglomeration cooled, the nipples fell out and the pot was fortunately undamaged. The young parents put the "object d'art" on the counter as a symbol of their inexperience.

Little Janelle could get into mischief, but her father was never too strict with her. Perhaps he remembered his and Claude's own mischievous youth when he wrote once to his mother, in 1970, that "Janelle does all kinds of mischief and tries to run away when she gets caught. She's always playing with the pots and pans in the cupboard and somehow manages to get her share of bumps on her head. She already had a black eye and managed to fall off the bed when I was watching her." She grew fast and was talking within the year, saying the usual Mommy and Daddy and also "no-no" whenever Ellison or Lorna changed her diaper or scolded her. "She is quite a 'copy-cat' now," her adoring father observed.

Being married to an officer, Lorna learned that military life was often a stressful series of accommodations and compromises. In college, she had grown dependent upon Ellison, and in their early married life she often relied upon her husband to make the decisions. She had given up her education for marriage, and at McClellan Air Force Base and later when they were to move to Edwards, she attempted to maintain a home, bring up Janelle and their second daughter, Darien, who was born in 1975, and pursue her degree. As Ellison's career blossomed and the military began to make demands upon his time, often giving him temporary duty away from his family, Lorna realized that she would need to take more responsibility for the family. "I had to learn to take

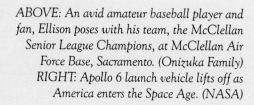

ABOVE: *An avid amateur baseball player and fan, Ellison poses with his team, the McClellan Senior League Champions, at McClellan Air Force Base, Sacramento. (Onizuka Family)*
RIGHT: *Apollo 6 launch vehicle lifts off as America enters the Space Age. (NASA)*

74

care of myself," she now recalls. "If the baby had to get a shot at the hospital, I had to do it alone. He was not there. Slowly you get accustomed to more independence."

After four successful years at McClellan Air Force Base, Ellison applied for and was accepted to the Air Force Test Pilot School at Edwards Air Force Base in the Mojave Desert, California. From August 1974 to July 1975 he completed his studies in formal academics and flying instruction in performance, stability and control, and systems flight testing of aircraft. He was not a pilot, nor did he formally have intentions of becoming one. Ellison was an experienced flight test engineer in the Air Force Test Pilot School. It was his responsibility to go up with the pilot and run tests on the aircraft while in flight to determine whether drawing board designs corresponded with aerospace realities. It was hardly a "safe" job since the aircraft were still undergoing design. More than one friend had been lost or maimed in accidents.

Air Force test pilots and engineers did not often think of the dangers of their work. They faced the risks on a daily basis, which were accepted as an emotional "given." In some ways, it was just a job and as Lorna recalls, "He never told us too much of the work. I did not worry too much." After test pilot school, Ellison was assigned to the Air Force Flight Test Center at Edwards. He served on the USAF Test Pilot School staff initially as a squadron flight test engineer and later as chief of the engineering support section in the training resources branch. His duties involved instruction of USAF Test Pilot School curriculum courses and management of all flight test modifications to general support fleet aircraft used by the school and flight test center. He logged more than 1,700 hours of flying time while serving in that capacity.

While flight test engineers were not permitted to fly the airplane, informally the pilot would sometimes let him play with the stick. The ground personnel never admitted that they knew, but Ellison would "catch a few thrills" quite often depending upon who was the pilot. He would play "touch

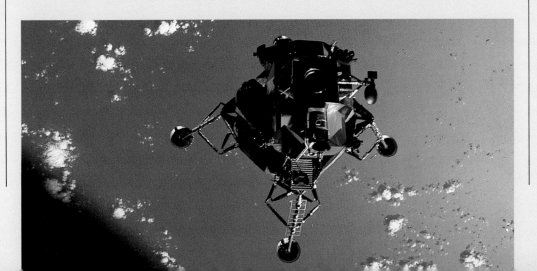

TOP: Bringing the pig out of the imu at a Hawaiian-style luau Ellison hosted at Edwards Air Force Base, California in 1975. ABOVE: Celebrating a Chinese New Year at Edwards Air Force Base, 1975. (Onizuka Family) LEFT: The test lunar lander Spider, photographed from its command module in March 1969. (NASA)

75

and go," landing and taking off. While in one sense Ellison's unbridled passion for flying was a self-indulgent pleasure, it was also a precautionary measure. If anything ever happened to the pilot, Ellison could always take over the controls.

As a consequence of the pressures they underwent and the isolation of living in the Mojave Desert, a certain camaraderie grew among the Air Force personnel at Edwards. They always enjoyed their "Friday Night Beer Busts" and on Saturday nights the couples would get together for their own partying. As Lorna says, Air Force couples had three choices: depression, divorce or fun. "We did not know how to get depressed, maybe we could not afford to get divorced, so we decided to have fun." The calendar was always filled with activities— working, bowling, golf and weekend parties. They also got involved in community activities just as they had done in Hawaii. Ellison was especially active in youth organizations. At Edwards and Sacramento he coached Little League baseball teams. During his last year at Edwards he was managing three teams of different age levels, one of which took second in the state championship play-offs.

He also found time for his daughters. Janelle, who during the years at Edwards was in elementary school, still vividly recalls the early mornings in the Mojave Desert when her father would jog with her before they went to work or school. He also got her interested in soccer, encouraging her to join the school team. "My dad would help me to stay in shape," she says, "with bike-riding, jogging and calisthenics. I would always run with my dad." And he tutored her in math—"he was great at math," his daughter proudly states.

As active as the years at Edwards were, there were moments of marital strain and stress. Ellison knew where his career was going—he was able to make changes and accept new conditions from the military. Lorna was responsible for the home and the stability of the family, which often was tested by the moves and uncertainties. Ellison would have to be away from home for long periods of time and the move to Edwards was a difficult adjustment for Lorna and the children. After four years in Sacramento, it was a hard assignment to leave for the isolation of the Mojave Desert. "I was no martyr," Lorna admits. "We had our spats." As much as everyone likes to believe they have the all-American family, Ellison and Lorna were more real and thus far more interesting than that. As is the case with husbands or wives who have strong career goals, the home is often sacrificed for their ambitions. Lorna needed to exert herself, to bring Ellison back to the focus of their family, and thus keep him rooted in a career that was to become dizzyingly hectic. She learned when to push, when to

OPPOSITE: *The dream of putting a permanent manned orbiting space station around the earth began in the early 1970's with the Skylab project. The space shuttle was to be the transport between earth and the space station. (NASA) ABOVE: Edwards Test Pilot School basketball team poses with their trophies, 1975. (Onizuka Family)*

Janelle's first Christmas, 1970 celebrated at
McClellan Air Force Base, Sacramento,
California. (Onizuka Family)

"Follow me and one day you'll be up there."

Janelle Onizuka is a bright, pretty young high school student who
has plans one day to go to college, perhaps majoring in business. She is also an
excellent soccer player. Some of her fondest memories of her father are the early
Mojave Desert mornings at Edwards Air Force Base when he would jog with her before
they went to work and school. He always helped her with her physical fitness and rarely
missed one of her soccer games. His bond of affection for both Janelle and Darien,
the youngest daughter, was paramount.

" When dad first came down, I never heard the end of him talking
about space. He told me it wasn't always dark up there—sometimes it was
a bright white. It's not always dark and it was really pretty.
The sky was sometimes even orange and yellow. You could see satellites.
He experimented with the macadamia nuts, putting them in the air
and trying to eat them. That's all he ever talked about.
"Follow me," he said, "and one day you'll be up there."

Going to NASA seems different now. Without Dad, I don't know that
place anymore. I wish I could do it all again, but its different. **"**

get hard, but promised him not to nag. "I would lose it sometimes," she would
later observe. "I'd tell him not to go on temporary duty. Sometimes I'd tell him
to go AWOL instead."

Was he the classic Japanese American husband who likes to think of
himself as a samurai and remain emotionless and uninvolved in family
matters—a bit of a male tyrant? "I teased him he was a shogun," Lorna answers,
"but he could push a vacuum cleaner. If there was something to do at home or
if he promised his friends a party, he would always help me." One year the
Onizukas hosted for their friends at Edwards a Hawaiian style luau. Although

78

the pig was baked in the oven and not an *imu*, or Hawaiian underground oven, it was a successful party that Ellison planned and helped execute.

What sustained the marriage, as it did his intense work, was the good-natured and even humor that Ellison brought to his family, friends and fellow workers. The smile that he wears in so many of his photographs was a natural expression off the camera—at social gatherings he always had a beer in his hand, a grin on his face, and an ability to make people feel comfortable. He had his own style of prankishness that was a touch outrageous but always good-natured. For example, while at Edwards one of the female test pilots, who had long blonde hair, was required to wear a short haired wig while on duty. She kept the wig in her locker, which was right above Ellison's. One morning she evidently had left her locker ajar, and when Ellison was banging his shut, the wig fell out on the floor. Screaming that it was "alive!" he feigned fear and began stomping it to death, cracking up all the other members of the squadron. Of course the poor wig was brutalized, and replaced in the locker to be found by an angry female pilot. But it was that sort of prankishness, perhaps from the outsider's point of view a bit cruel, that kept men and women who daily risked their lives, sane with tension-releasing laughter. Most of the squadron at McClellan Air Force Base also remember the day when Ellison, jealous because Lorna never had time in the morning to fix him a noon meal, epoxied all the crew's lunchpails tightly shut!

As good-natured as Ellison was, he retained a sharp edge of temper, especially when his ambitions came up against inefficiency or sloppiness. In an uncharacteristic burst of anger in a letter he wrote to his mother while still at Sacramento, Ellison threatened to write to the Hawaii County Chief of Police accusing him and his department of ineptitude. Evidently, while at McClellan Air Force Base, Ellison needed a Hawaii driver's license to operate a vehicle. His temporary license had expired and his GI license was useless without proof of his Hawaii document. The Kona motor vehicle department had not sent the license and his commanding officer wanted to know what was going on. Ellison asked his mother to help him out before he got into trouble. "I'll write to the Chief of Police or someone in the gov't 'cause I'm not going to take the blame," he added at the end of his letter. "If they couldn't get the license to me before the temporary one expired, they could at least write me a letter or another temporary one, 'cause I did my share of going back to renew my old one!" He was no pushover, no matter how good-natured.

While Ellison and Lorna settled down to military life, raised a family, endured their problems and enjoyed their social life, an idea was being born

Graduation from Edward's Test Pilot School, 1975. (Onizuka Family)

that would transform their existence. In the sixties, the American space program had been a tremendous national success. After the fear of being left behind by Russian sputniks, American energy and know-how was redirected to "catching up and surpassing" the Soviets in space. "Space is the new ocean," declared President John F. Kennedy in the early sixties, "and this nation must sail upon it." The Mercury program successfully orbited the first Americans in tiny capsules. That program was followed by the two-man Gemini missions and then four Apollo flights before Astronauts Neil Armstrong, Edwin Aldrin and Michael Collins went into lunar orbit in July 1969 and miraculously walked on the moon.

NASA, looking beyond the manned moon flights, directed its attention in the early '70's to an orbiting space station, a Skylab serviced by a large space truck that would be able to ferry large crews and heavy payloads into space. Thus in 1972 was born the NASA project which would "take the astronomical costs out of astronautics" and would turn the "space frontier of the 1970's into familiar territory." The winged orbiter or "space shuttle" would be capable of at least a hundred missions into space. Launched by its own three engines and large external booster rockets that would separate after lift-off, the 100-ton shuttle would maneuver in space with the assistance of the three engines. Rather than falling back to earth, the shuttle would fly back into the atmosphere and, using its wings, return to earth like a giant glider.

After the Apollo moon missions, the recruitment of astronauts had stopped—there was no need for a new crop of young test pilots who had the "right stuff" for dangerous space exploration. But the shuttle was to need a new generation of men and women who were physically fit, mentally alert and capable of a wide range of skills beyond just flying. For the space shuttle would need a complex crew of pilots and payload and mission specialists who, working as a team, could explore the possibilities of long-term travel in space hundreds of miles above the earth. So in 1977 the word went out within the ranks of the military and civilian aeronautic organizations—NASA was again recruiting for astronauts. In a Tennessee hotel room, a young Japanese American flight test engineer from Kona on temporary duty away from his assignment at Edwards Air Force Base, called long distance to his secretary. The deadline was approaching, and he wanted to submit his application and vitae to NASA for the job of astronaut. It would mean long hours of typing and preparation, but could she get it in on time?

For her successful efforts, Ellison would send her a large bouquet of flowers.

OPPOSITE: *The achievement of a century—man walks on the moon. Astronaut James B. Irwin of Apollo 15 mission gives a military salute while standing beside the lunar module "Falcon." ABOVE: The Propwash Award—for coolness under pressure, a sense of humor and high morale, given to Ellison Onizuka at Edward's Test Pilot School. OVERLEAF: The shuttle Challenger is ferried to Florida on a NASA 747 for its maiden flight. (NASA)*

CHAPTER SIX

The Class of '78

Astronaut candidate Ellison Onizuka in survival school at Vance Air Force Base, Oklahoma, in August, 1978. He is being helped into a parachute harness in preparation for exercises in being ejected from an aircraft. (NASA)

Ellison had been in Tennessee for about three weeks in 1977 on temporary duty when he called Lorna with the news that he had decided to submit his astronaut application to NASA. He had also called his secretary, he explained, and was having her help him type up the necessary papers. It was just a shot in the dark, he led Lorna to believe, a last minute decision for which he was rushing to get all the paperwork in on time. His secretary was being worked to death on this, and he asked Lorna if she'd get her a bouquet of flowers. He was hoping against hope that from among the thousands of applications being sent in, just possibly he would have a chance to be selected.

NASA's announcement that it was recruiting a new team of astronauts for the "space shuttle" program was the opportunity Ellison had been waiting for to fulfill his boyhood dreams of space travel. Up until that time it seemed that astronauts were experienced pilots fitting a particular physical, if not racial, mold. But the shuttle program was consciously recruiting a broad spectrum of backgrounds and types—pilots, engineers, scientists and specialists of all races and both sexes. While it was a long shot, there was still the chance that with his excellent flight test engineer record he would be considered for the program. After announcing to Lorna that he had submitted his application, they did not talk about it much. With all the activities, work and socializing, who had time to talk about a little thing like going into space?

As the months went by, Lorna even forgot about the application. Then NASA announced that after reviewing nearly 8,000 candidates, 220 would be interviewed for selection. Ellison Onizuka's name was among the 220. After making the cut, Ellison felt good about it, but the couple never actually celebrated each step towards his final selection. In the tight-knit community of Edwards Air Force Base and among the personnel of the Test Pilot School, there were many men and women who had not been as fortunate. One did not celebrate other people's disappointments.

The 220 men and women who had survived this cut were then invited to Houston for an extensive physical and round of interviewing. As NASA official George Abbey described the process, "we are really looking for two kinds of astronauts: Pilots who can fly very well and learn to fly the orbiter; and mission specialists who have an engineering or science background who hopefully have operational experience, and who have the desire to do many things well. They must also want to fly in space." From the first interview, Abbey and other NASA administrators were impressed by the young Japanese American officer. He had an excellent record of preparation for the space program. His engineering degree from the University of Colorado, his Air Force experience and his involvement in the Test Pilot School at Edwards (no small achievement in itself) were excellent references for the shuttle program. In the interview he was articulate, confident and stood out as someone who was well thought of and respected. He had helped to improve the curriculum at the Test Pilot School and was an admired teacher.

He also passed his physical examination with flying colors. Because NASA was encouraging a new kind of applicant that was an astronaut/engineer/scientist, they had relaxed many of the physical requirements for the job. Instead of the previous 5 foot 11 inch restriction, anyone between 5 feet 6 inches and 6 feet was eligible. At 5 foot 9 inches and 162 pounds, Ellison now met the physical qualifications. As he later explained to his mother, he had also confessed to the doctors about an earlier back injury. One summer while visiting home from college, his father had gotten him a job at the Captain Cook Building Supply Company. Lifting a heavy object, he strained his back, so he drove himself to a Portuguese woman in Honaunau named Mrs. Lyda Rapoza, who applied a folk remedy. Cupping his back, she massaged him until he felt fully recovered. NASA examiners could find no evidence of the injury, concluding, as one doctor told him, "that lady must have done a good job." He would be sure to later tell his mother of the incident—she always was told when he passed a physical. "Good," she would answer, "or else you can't go flying."

ABOVE: *Father and daughters, Janelle and Darien, play in a friend's pool in Houston, 1978. (Onizuka Family) RIGHT: Ellison straps into a NASA T-38 aircraft. Although he never flew airplanes, he always enjoyed the opportunity to go aloft in frequent flights on the T-38. (NASA)*

"He had the right kind of background and desire to get into the program," Abbey recalls. "He was one we did not have any trouble identifying or selecting right away." Of course, when Ellison returned to Edwards, he had no idea that he had done so well in the interviews. In fact, he was quite humbled and discouraged. NASA had shown all the candidates the Johnson Space Center at Houston and he had the opportunity to meet the other men and women. Returning home, he was suddenly talking quite candidly about his earnestness in wanting to be selected for the program, but admitted to Lorna that he felt a little inadequate. There were so many excellent candidates that NASA wouldn't make a mistake if it selected any one of them. For one of the first times she could remember, the smiling, aggressive flight test engineer faltered in his determination and confidence. "He came home humbled," Lorna observes, "still hoping but really humbled." In a way, she notes, he was also relieved of some of the competitive pressures. Whatever the decision, the program would be made up of highly qualified, competent people.

Thirty-five men and women were named in January of 1978 to become what was to be called the Class of '78—a group of dedicated astronauts that would train for America's pioneer efforts to bring space closer to earth. They would be the generation of star voyagers to almost make flying out to the stars an ordinary, daily event as simple as riding an airplane. NASA had plans for politicians, newspaper journalists, teachers and ordinary citizens to eventually join the astronauts, symbolizing that space travel had come of age. The telephone calls went out from NASA headquarters and newspapers were alerted throughout the nation.

Ellison was riding a bus from his home to his office the morning NASA tried to inform him of his selection. Lorna had to use the family car that morning, so Ellison took the base bus, which stopped at each pick up point and seemed to always take forever to get to its destination. NASA had tried to call his office and then called Lorna at home. She explained the situation so officials tried his office again. When he walked in, some of his fellow workers who had also been interviewed for the job already had their answers. Immediately, Ellison figured he had been turned down, since he had received no such call. Then his secretary informed him it was NASA on the line. Everyone waited anxiously to get the word whether Onizuka was now an astronaut or not. When he hung the phone up, his face lit with a smile and he gave the traditional thumbs up!

Thousands of miles away Claude Onizuka was driving to his office where he was a manager of the Kona Community Federal Credit Union, Kailua

The astronaut candidate in the parachute harness at survival school, Vance Air Force Base, 1978. (NASA)

A shuttle orbiter is being hoisted onto the back of a NASA 747 at the mate-demate facility at Dryden Flight Research Center at Edwards Air Force Base in California. (NASA)

Branch. Suddenly the radio news announced that Ellison Onizuka of Keopu, Kona had been one of thirty-five astronauts to be selected for NASA's space shuttle program. Claude knew his brother was at Edwards Air Force Base, but he never fully realized that Ellison was trying to become an astronaut. When he got to the office he called his mother and sister Shirley, but both lines were busy. So many newspaper reporters were trying to get a call in, that everyone's lines were tied up. Finally Claude got through to his mother and asked "What's going on?" Only much later that evening was Ellison able to get through the busy lines.

In Honolulu, Ellison's sister Norma Sakamoto suddenly found herself a television star—she had heard the news when a local station called her at her office asking for an on-the-spot interview. She got clearance from her boss at Hawaiian Trust and the TV news staff crowded into the tiny data processing area over which she was then manager. Representative Dan Akaka flew from Honolulu to Kona when he heard the news. Here was a young man from his congressional district and he felt it an honor and duty to congratulate the mother. He remembers being driven to a little mama- and papa-san store in mauka Kona. Nobody was in the store so he went around to the back area where the house was and called out for Mrs. Onizuka. He heard a tiny voice answer "I'll be right up." He introduced himself and told her he was so proud that Ellison had been selected as an astronaut. "She was so happy," the Congressman recalls. "She told me a little about how he had applied for it, and about how hard he had worked on the application." No matter how well known or important the person, Mrs. Onizuka always treated him as if he was just a neighbor sitting on the store's front porch.

Back at Edwards Air Force Base, as the Onizukas of Kona were becoming state celebrities overnight and having to cope with all the media attention, Ellison and Lorna were having their own adjustments to make. The phone, young Janelle can still recall, was ringing off the hook. "When I found out he was going to be an astronaut," she says, "I answered the phone every two seconds. It was exciting." It was less exciting for Lorna. That day she had used the car to go to the dentist and have a wisdom tooth pulled. She was hardly in the partying mood, but some friends brought a bottle of champagne which they emptied.

In their training, new astronauts become acquainted with all aspects of flight operations. At Houston's Johnson Space Center, Ellison, Judy Resnick and Steve Hawley listen to a briefing on mission control center functions in the mission control room. (NASA)

He Belonged to Everybody

As close-knit as his family was, the fame and busy schedule which marked Ellison Onizuka's life as an astronaut often took him away from his family. Norma Sakamoto, one of Ellison's older sisters, was interviewed in her office at the Hawaiian Trust Company in Honolulu where she is a manager. Having moved away from Kona after her marriage, Norma understood the difficulties of separating oneself from one's family. For Ellison, the separation was often beyond his control. He had become an important Island hero and had therefore sacrificed his own time for family and relaxation.

" It wasn't easy for any of us at the beginning suddenly being in the limelight. We had to get used to it. He wasn't just part of the family, he belonged to everybody at that point. It took longer for my mom to understand that. She wanted her son home, but there were always speaking engagements and news coverage. NASA would arrange interviews for him in Honolulu and he couldn't stay long in Kona. It of course wasn't his doing. He said he'd like to come home unnoticed. But there was always media. Somehow they would find out.

Sometimes you'd say to yourself, "He's still the same person." He changed a little bit but when he came home he was just like the local people. He knew how he'd have to be when he was away. Sometimes you could tell he was trying to keep everything like it used to be before the astronaut program. We used to tease each other. We'd say, "It's not like you're part of the family" and he'd answer, "I am!" "

89

The Onizuka home in Houston, Texas.

It was, as Lorna says, a "bittersweet" feeling with the news of Ellison's selection. The "squadron" at Test Pilot School was socially and emotionally close and Ellison admired many of the men that got turned down for the job. A few of his friends at Edwards did get selected, among them Dick Scobee, Steve Nagel, Brewster Shaw and Loren Shriver, who would later be the pilot on Ellison's first space flight. But still the celebrating was toned down in respect to those who were disappointed. It was not until all those who had been selected as astronauts had their farewell party that there was any real celebration.

The next few months were a mixture of exhausting media attention, tying up loose ends and preparing for a new move, this time to Houston. Again, it was difficult for the family to sever ties with the friends they had made at Edwards, but at least a few of them were going to train at the Johnson Space Center together. In a series of letters to his mother in the months before the move to Houston in June, 1978, Ellison described the excitement but also the pressures that were mounting. He and Lorna had purchased their first house in Houston, in a new subdivision called Meadow Green, about a mile and a half from the Johnson Space Center. The down payment had taken most of their savings, but the house was a large four bedroom, two and one-half bath

90

structure which was within a mile of Janelle's elementary school. They had not yet found a preschool for Darien. Ellison was looking forward to putting a small yard in the back where he could do gardening. There was much work to be done to transfer his Test School position to his successor.

The prospects of being able to afford one more visit to Hawaii before their new NASA life seemed unlikely. They had very little cash after the down payment and there was furniture and other items to purchase for their new home. But the Onizukas had always been a close family, supporting each other and helping out so that the family could have some time together. Mrs. Onizuka must have been disappointed at the prospects of not seeing Ellison, Lorna and the kids, and offered to bring them home. "Please don't think that our first thoughts were not to come home before going to Texas," Ellison wrote to his mother. "Our first ideas were to go home before going to Texas because it was a dream come true for me and it'll probably be two or more years before we could go home again." Mrs. Onizuka had planned to go with a church group to Brazil that summer, but instead brought her boy and his family home.

Having come home for their visit and then returning to Houston, the family settled in to the new life in Texas. For the first time in their marriage, the Onizukas were living in a civilian community. Lorna had to make lots of little adjustments—like relearning how to shop at a supermarket instead of the base commissary. Most of the neighbors were non-Texan transplants; some were civilians like Ron McNair, a fellow minority-group astronaut. Lorna decided that she would once again attempt to finish her college education that had been interrupted so many times by the responsibilities of home. She resumed her four year degree program in clinical psychology, taking night classes on the nights Ellison was sure to be home. "Sometimes we have a schedule that people don't believe," he wrote home, "but the girls are always taken care of and we manage to get everything done."

It did not take long for Ellison and Lorna to also become deeply involved in community activities in a style not unlike that they had in Sacramento and Edwards Air Force Base. Although his time was restricted due to his training hours and NASA responsibilities, Ellison made time for his daughters' extracurricular activities. Janelle and a grown-up Darien were both soccer players—their father was a charter member of the soccer booster club and helped in their tournaments. He and Lorna were active in the Houston Livestock Show and Rodeo International Committee. These organizations were similar to the 4-H Club and Future Farmers of America that Ellison had known as a young teenager. "There are hundreds of people in our area," NASA

Ellison is fitted for a space suit at Houston's Johnson Space Center, November 1979. (Onizuka Family)

91

administrator George Abbey recalls of the impact Ellison had on people, "who met Ellison only a couple of times but who remember him and thought he was genuinely interested in them."

The Class of '78, though, had little time for outside activities, especially their first year of training. All the class—pilots and mission specialists—received much the same preparation. Classes in oceanography, astronomy, basic science, computers and mathematics were required. Simulated training in weightlessness, "zero gravity" conditions, and becoming accustomed with equipment and pressurized space suits were fundamental. Crews were assembled and put through the simulation of take-off over and over again. Every conceivable scenario was thrown at them to see their reactions during the critical lift-off period. How did they react? What would have been a better reaction? Alternatives were tested, discussed and retested.

In addition to their training as a team, the shuttle astronauts were also given special training according to their perceived orbiter responsibility. As Ellison explained in a letter to his mother in April 1979, "My training is continuing at a pretty good pace and the technical projects, speaking assignments and other jobs keep us pretty busy. I've been assigned to work on NASA's Solid Spinning Upper Stage (SSUS) as a technical assignment." Already NASA had recognized in Ellison an astronaut who made excellent presentations, representing NASA in the best possible light, often volunteering his time to speak to civic organizations and school groups. "I've given a few short tours of the Johnson Space Center to some of the distinguished visitors to NASA JSC," he wrote his mother "and a bunch of interviews for newspapers and TV/Radio." NASA was also aware of his critical role in relations with Japan. "In the past months I've talked to quite a few of the press from Japan." A loyal and loving member of the NASA team, he wrote that "Hopefully it helped the people there and did some good for NASA."

The men and women sometimes worked eighty-hour weeks and were put through physical and emotional pressure. It is little wonder, then, that they became a team that was interwoven emotionally and socially. On Fridays the camaraderie seen at college and Edwards was continued for Ellison with Happy Hours. Being in Texas, there were also the traditional Chili Cookoffs. "Ellison got to be the very best judge of chili," George Abbey recalls. The Class of '78 could release their tensions with intense partying. They knew how to consume their beer when the opportunity allowed it. For there was always the unspoken presence of danger that surrounded all of their work and common destiny. Everyone knew that the shuttle was a highly complicated piece of machinery

An interior view of the vertical assembly building showing the mating of an orbiter vehicle to the external fuel tank and the solid rocket boosters. (NASA)

CHAPTER SEVEN
"The Ride of a Lifetime"

One of the sixteen sunrises seen from the orbiter Columbia during its first historic flight. (NASA)

ape Canaveral becomes like a massive human beehive as a shuttle mission countdown approaches. Thousands of technicians putting in long hours swarm around the launch pad, checking and rechecking the final details of what is the most intricate and largest piece of aerodynamic machinery ever devised. Liquid hydrogen and oxygen is pumped into the massive fuel tank and the two roman candle booster rockets are tested. The payload is carefully weighed and positioned in the shuttle orbiter as the last preparations are completed. The crewmembers, following their own preparations and final briefing, are quarantined one week before the launch. Their isolation is to minimize their exposure to germs—an ill astronaut in space can seriously endanger the mission.

The process of preparing for a shuttle mission is exhaustive. During the pre-launch days of STS-1, the first mission, Ellison was working seventy-two hours straight. He once came home at 3:00 a.m. to find Lorna and some of the astronaut wives sitting in the living room. He was drained and his eyes had begun hemorrhaging. Lorna, concerned for his health, scolded him for driving himself so hard. "I remember him telling me," Lorna says, "that there were people in the firing room, whom I would never know, but they were working longer then he was." It was so typical of Ellison, Lorna recalls, to strive harder in appreciation for those who were also going the extra mile. "There were always people working harder than I was," he told his wife. "I have no right to complain."

The excitement of launch is compounded by the fact that at times it seems the momentum of the nation is swirling towards Cape Canaveral. Reporters, friends, dignitaries, well-wishers, television cameras and onlookers are focusing on all the curious human details, the condition of the tiles, the diet of the astronauts and the feelings of the families. Telegrams flood in from across the country, interviews for the press are convened, and hot, bright television lights are turned on the wife and children. "Do you ever worry about the danger?" "What are your feelings about your father being an astronaut?" "How will it feel to be the first woman astronaut to fly in space?" "Does being the first Asian American astronaut make you feel special?" The questions are mostly well-intentioned, but they become relentless and as exhausting as any other flight preparation routine.

The flight of *Discovery* in January 1985 aroused both special preparation and attention. It was to be the fifteenth shuttle mission in four years and the first fully classified American manned military space flight. For the first time in

At the top of the page is a reproduction of a scroll bearing many handwritten signatures.

over two decades of manned space flights, NASA determined to keep all communications between the crew and ground control secret. The exact date and time of the launch would be concealed. Most on-board activities during flight were to be kept confidential even after landing.

Two important research projects, of an unclassified nature, were to be carried by flight STS-51C. The first was an Australian research experiment to investigate the effects of different diseases on red blood cell aggregation and blood viscosity. "Aggregation of Red Blood Cells" explored the effect of weightlessness on normal and eight varieties of diseased red blood cells, including heart disease, hypertension, diabetes and cancer. The only involvement required of the crew during flight was the flipping of a process switch to activate the experiment during the first twenty-four hours after launch. The second research experiment was to determine the effects of weightlessness on the transference of a liquid from one tank to another. "The Fluid Management Demonstration," sponsored by NASA and the Air Force, was intended to study the transfer of fluids planned for servicing and maintaining spacecraft in orbit. Both projects had been slated for earlier shuttle flights but due to weight considerations had been postponed to STS-51C. They were carried in the mid-deck lockers in the space shuttle's crew cabin.

STS-51C also had the distinction of being the first shuttle to carry an Asian American and a native son of Hawaii into space. The media had focused attention on the women and ethnic minorities that comprised the Class of '78. When Sally Ride became the first American woman in space, the national hoopla was intense. Although Asian Americans had far less public clout than women, Ellison Onizuka similarly became something of a "hero" for Japanese Americans on the mainland and in Hawaii. It was a role he evidently wore with some uneasiness. Growing up in the rural backcountry of Kona, the young

ABOVE: A pin showing the crew of Discovery, flight STS-51C. RIGHT: The scroll signed by the hundreds of residents of Kona wishing their astronaut native son "good luck" on his first space flight.

Ellison had learned to see himself simply as a member of a culturally diverse community. The idea of ethnicity, of his "Japaneseness," was an accepted but not exaggerated image of himself. His explorer scout upbringing and later military experiences had instilled a patriotic Americanism which he felt overrode any ethnic differences. When reporters first asked him how it felt to be an Asian American minority, he answered "I didn't know I was a minority." Lorna, who was sitting at his side at the time, remembers dropping her mouth in disbelief and Ellison giving her a watchful eye suggesting she watch what she say next. Obviously he was aware of his ethnic roots, but he was attempting to make a larger point which he had learned in the multicultural world of Kona.

In Hawaii, the excitement over Ellison Onizuka's flight into space was less directed towards his ethnicity than the fact that he was a "local boy" who had earned national prominence. Kona, of course, was jubilant. At a Kona District Scouting Recognition Banquet, former Scoutmaster Norman Sakata read a letter from Ellison thanking "all the fine people back home who made it possible" for him to become an astronaut. Then everyone in attendance signed a twelve-foot-long scroll—more than 140 signatures and personal messages were recorded and the scroll was sent to Ellison. Mayor Dante Carpenter's staff sent to the crew a gift package of non-perishable island products and a congratulatory message. *The Honolulu Advertiser* called Major Ellison Onizuka "Hawaii's

ABOVE: *A cartoon that was pinned to an office wall in NASA depicting the oft-delayed crew of the secret DOD mission waiting "in prison" for their "go-ahead."* LEFT: *The crew of the Discovery, flight STS-51C. From left to right, Mission Specialist Onizuka, Lt. Col. Loren Shriver, Commander T. K. Mattingly, Mission Specialist Jim Buchli and Payload Specialist Gary Payton. (NASA)*

program moving again." In the course of his legislative work, he had the opportunity to meet Ellison many times in Washington. When he learned that Ellison was going to fly to Kauai for a brief training session at the space tracking station at Kokee, he arranged that Ellison's mother would be able to attend a benefit luau being given the astronaut by the men there. Ellison would not have otherwise had time to go home to Kona on the hectic schedule.

Ellison had asked Representative Akaka to witness his first space flight in 1985 and invited him to have dinner with the quarantined crew on the evening of January 22, the night before the scheduled lift-off. By 9:00 p.m. the blood tests and physical examination were completed and the Congressman was ushered into the crew quarters. Shriver and Ellison, with Lorna, welcomed him into a large reception room lined with maps. Photographs were taken, official STS-51C patches were given to the Congressman and Ellison took the lead in making him feel right at home. "I saw Ellison as a truly Hawaii-nurtured person," Representative Akaka recalls of the dinner. "He showed a lot of humility. He brought me a chair…he looked after me."

After a short conversation, Commander Mattingly entered from the side and, as was characteristic for the prank-loving crew, fired a blank shell from a pistol. "Dinner is served," he calmly announced. In the next room was a chicken dinner served in first class style. In the middle of the table was a cake decorated to resemble the shuttle flight patch. All the crew and their wives attended the dinner. "Guess what?" he at one point asked the Congressman. "I'm taking up with me Kona coffee and macadamia nuts. We are going to drink and eat them up there." Ellison was to carry with him into space a few other special remembrances including patches of the 442nd Combat Regiment Team and the 100th Battalion, both of whom he admired for their wartime courage in proving the loyalty of Japanese Americans. He also wore the Buddhist medallion that his father had bought for him after he had lost the first in the sand many years before.

That night, however, was incredibly cold, causing concern among NASA technicians. Antifreeze in great quantities was taken to the launch pad to keep the water lines open as the midnight temperature had dropped below thirty degrees. Emergency water lines were frozen, fittings cracked and a frozen oxygen tank valve delayed the work. Large chunks of ice, it was feared, would form on the external fuel tank and during lift-off would fall off and damage the shuttle orbiter. "I can never remember the day before a launch being this cold," a concerned chief astronaut John Young announced to the press. The flight launch was postponed until January 24th, hoping for warmer weather.

A Smile from Ear to Ear

Astronaut Robert "Hoot" Gibson shared an office with Ellison Onizuka at NASA's
Houston headquarters. They graduated from the shuttle mission's first training school,
notably the "Class of '78." They played baseball together, pulled pranks on one another
and enjoyed more than one Happy Hour after a long work week. They shared
a common winning spirit. The astronaut was interviewed after
the Punchbowl memorial service in Honolulu.

" *There is one photograph of Ellison that I'll always remember.*
It's the one where he's getting into an airplane wearing a parachute. He has
a smile from ear to ear. I think that is the way I'll always picture him. That
smile. He had a completely infectious smile. He would squint his eyes up
and they'd squish together when he was smiling at you. That is the way I'll
picture him. The way we'll always think of him. A good friend. I don't
recall if I ever heard a bad word out of him for anybody. He was a humble,
capable person. Very hardworking person who just couldn't seem to do
anything wrong to anyone. That's how we'll picture him.
He's really going to be missed. If he wasn't the best, he was one of the best.
We are really losing out by not having Ellison. **"**

The precise time of the takeoff remained a secret, to be announced
nineteen minutes before launch. The Department of Defense reversed an
earlier decision and allowed NASA to erect a large electronic counter for the
convenience of the visitors in the viewing stands four miles away. By 1:15 p.m.
EST the families and friends learned that the countdown was going smoothly.
The air had warmed up and the sky was beautifully clear. The Hawaii
delegation began to joke that Ellison was to be credited for the great weather—
"Hawaiian weather courtesy of Hawaii's first astronaut." The temperature had
risen from twenty-four degrees on Monday to sixty-six degrees on Tuesday. At
2:50 p.m. the engines of the giant rockets were fired and the shuttle *Discovery*

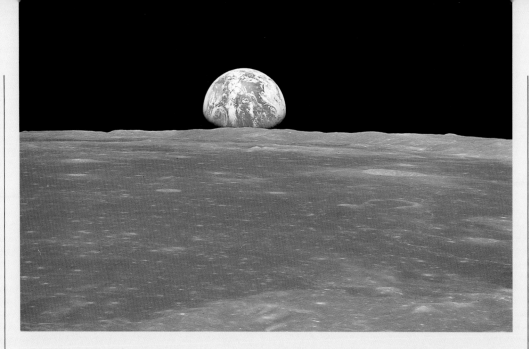

with her five-man crew lifted up towards the stars, its glorious orange fire scorching the sky like spectacular fireworks. If he could have looked out a window towards the viewing stands, Hawaii's first astronaut would have seen his Kona family and friends holding a great banner that simply read ONIZUKA '85.

Every astronaut has their own style in describing their feelings during those first 8.5 minutes of ascent. Most stress that words are never enough to express the emotion, the quickened adrenaline and overwhelming exhilaration that they feel going from 0 to 2,000 mph in one minute! Ellison would later describe the sensation as lots of shaking, vibrations and loud knocking, like metal bouncing against metal. The noise, he noted, was far louder than what he had expected from the simulated launches that the crews had undergone during training. "There are no surprises," Ellison explained, "but the intensity is higher."

At launching, Captain Mattingly, who was in space twice before, lay back in *Discovery's* left side commander's seat. To his right was copilot Lieutenant Colonel Loren Shriver. Both men had visual sightings skyward as the machine rose towards orbit. In their aft flight deck positions, mission specialists Buchli and Onizuka were not able to look outside, but were busy monitoring the operation of the orbiter. Payload specialist Payton rode through the ascent in his seat on the mid-deck. Ellison was responsible for safety systems but, in the shock and pressure of lift-off, it was often difficult to keep one's attention on gauges. "It was like putting a heavy barrel on your chest," he once described lift-off to his sister Norma. "You feel as if you are going to be squashed. But it's a good feeling."

Colonel Shriver later described the ascent in his cool, descriptive manner: "Seven seconds before the lift-off, it really gets serious. The main engines start to fire up. Within three seconds of lift-off they are at full speed. You can really feel it, the rumbling and shaking. The shuttle is bent forward a little and then comes back. Then the back boosters fire. That is a very dynamic sensation for about two minutes. The ship shakes and rattles. The noise is loud but muffled within the crew cabin which is insulated and pressurized. Plus you have your earphones and helmet on which muffles the noise. On the intercom you talk among yourselves, keeping the crew on the mid-deck appraised of what goes on, since they cannot see out of the shuttle. The really dynamic shaking and buffeting is due to the main boosters firing for two minutes until the fuel is burned up and they are jettisoned. From then on it gets smoother as the main engines accelerate. The whole ascent is eight and one-half minutes from lift-off to main engine shutdown. You go from zero velocity to 25,600 feet/second, or Mach 26."

"Hoot" Gibson, who flew the tenth shuttle mission and was Ellison's office mate, describes the same process in his own words: "Lifting off the launch pad, it feels like a catapult shot. It is close to two times the force of gravity when you lift off. Of course, you can't feel that. The fastest car you've been in or jet, cannot accelerate at two times the force of gravity. So it is a real kick when that thing lifts off. And it is deceiving how fast it is accelerating because it is so big. When you see it lift off the launch pad and by the time it gets to the top of the launch pad you are going one hundred miles per hour already, but it doesn't look like it. Then you go through the roll maneuver and you can see the beaches nearby and a lot of shaking starts from the solid rocket motors. They put out a lot of vibration. The acceleration is so fast, the air density is decreasing and the wind pressure is getting greater as you go up to 36,000 feet. That gives you shaking from the wind. Then when you get to where the jet stream is, 35,000 feet, the vehicle steers into the wind to minimize the load so that there is a lot of rumbling and shaking. The noise is surprisingly getting less as you go. The noise is greatest when you are right on the ground where the sound waves can reflect off the ground and come right back up. At some point you get completely out of the atmosphere and you can't hear anything. You have a million and a half pounds of engines burning behind you and you have no sound. Within twenty seconds the sky is starting to turn black. You are traveling at 2,000 miles per hour and it is a real experience. I remembered that when we got to the main engine cutoff on my first flight. You've just gone through the most stressful portion of the ascent; you're all keyed up with little

The first Asian American in manned space flight wearing a distinctive headband, floats "weightless" in Discovery. (NASA)

ABOVE: Ellison's jump suit with the patch of the Discovery DOD mission. RIGHT: Ellison and Loren Shriver floating "weightless" in Discovery. (NASA) OPPOSITE: Astronauts Dale Gardner and Joe Allen maneuver a satellite into its berth outside the shuttle Discovery. (NASA)

time for malfunctions and you are suddenly floating in orbit. I suddenly relaxed and got a great big smile on my face and I said, 'That was some ride. Let's do that again!'"

One of the regrets Ellison would always have about that first flight was that it was classified. There was very little he could say about what went on. Later, one of his friends, for example, would innocently ask him how high he was flying above the earth. "Next question," Ellison quickly replied. NASA blocked out most all of the transmissions from the orbiter, communicating with the crew in code or simply to say that all systems were working well. It was announced that the orbiter was flying over one hundred and fifteen miles above the earth and making one rotation every ninety minutes. Colonel Shriver reported also that the crew had seen the large one hundred fifty-four foot external fuel tank reenter the atmosphere and disintegrate. "It was a brilliant display of fireworks," Shriver reported to NASA.

The flight was scheduled for four days and the press tried to get as much information as possible concerning what was going on in the *Discovery*. NASA limited the news to stories about how the controllers in Houston thanked Ellison for the Kona coffee and macadamia nuts he left for them. Captain Mattingly said that the orbiter's systems were so stable that "it makes you think the gauges are printed on here." And in one personal transmission, Colonel Shriver passed on an anniversary greeting to his wife of seventeen years, Diane. Other than those tidbits, the only solid news of the day was that for the first time in any shuttle launch, Soviet fishing trawlers had *not* been in the Cape area at the time of lift-off.

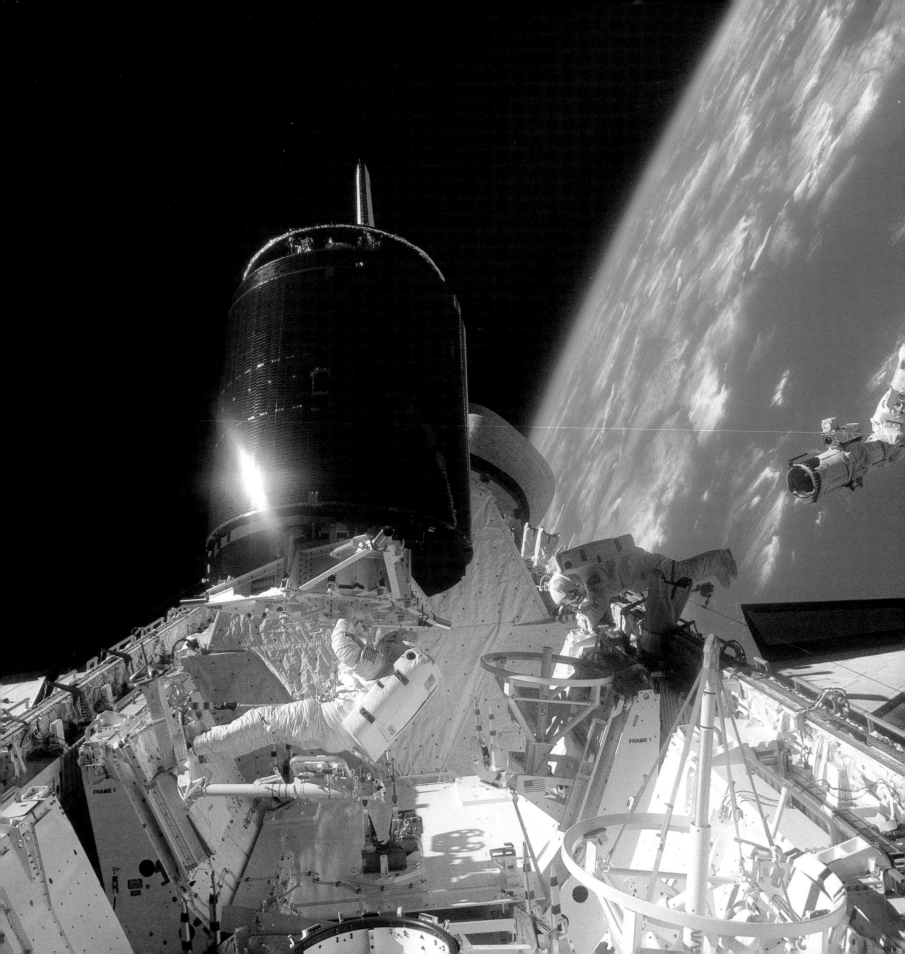

Aboard the *Discovery* the crew was experiencing what Ellison would later call a "fantastic experience." "What a view of earth!" he later remarked. "I highly recommend it to everybody. It's a beautiful planet. It is the most beautiful sight you'll ever see, something that film just can't capture." The weightlessness also impressed him. "Once you experience what the weightless environment affords, you can really appreciate what that medium can do for you," he said. "You need to hold on to something or hook your feet or legs or you'll just go floating away. I was surprised to see eating and everything like that is not as difficult as it would seem to be. But how you manage the food is very important. You wouldn't sprinkle salt or pepper on the food because it would just float away too."

On the third day of flight, the crew received the bad news—what was to be a short flight would be even shorter. Instead of the planned four days, the *Discovery* was ordered to return to earth to avoid a storm headed for the Florida coast. The directive came but sixteen hours before touchdown. On the forty-seventh orbit, Captain Mattingly, viewing the Cape from their position in space, relayed to ground the sentiments that the crew was "obviously not ready to come home." Apparently joking about the secretive nature of the flight, the Captain also reported that in spite of what they say about the good weather at the Cape, as he passed over he noticed a stealth cloud just off to the left of the field. He said it may not show up yet but it's there.

The descent of the orbiter began with a blast from the twin braking rockets at 3:16 p.m. EST while the ship cruised 17,500 mph over the Indian Ocean. The shuttle passed over the Gulf of Mexico coastline, south of New Orleans then crossed over Florida and made a broad left turn over the Cape landing north to south. The Cape Canaveral landing was described as "real beautiful," by younger brother Claude. "It came in real smooth, just like a regular commercial airliner." The time was 4:23 p.m. EST (11:23 a.m. Hawaii time) on Sunday, January 27th. *Discovery* touched down at the Kennedy Space Center's 15,000 foot landing strip three days, one hour and thirty-three minutes after it had blasted off. It was the fourth shuttle landing at the Florida space facilities.

Later Ellison would address a group of students at his alma mater, the University of Colorado. Exclaiming that the space flight was "something I've always wanted to do," he admitted that "everything I've done has been deliberately to apply to become an astronaut." The experience now over, he said "I have to pinch myself to see if this is real." But as he described the shuttle flight, it was "the ride of a lifetime."

Ellison demonstrates the use of chopsticks in "weightless" space for the benefit of his fellow crew members on flight STS-51C. (NASA)

Other than spouses, family and friends were not allowed to see or talk to the astronauts immediately upon their return to earth. After descending the stairs from the shuttle, the astronauts waved to a small group of onlookers and inspected the ship before leaving in an "astrovan" for their quarters. Later that Sunday, the crew and their wives flew on to their homes in Houston in a twin-engine NASA airplane where they would be reunited with their children, friends and family. The Hawaii delegation flew to Houston the next day for the celebration and a tour of the Johnson Space Center.

When her son safely landed, Mrs. Onizuka remembers clapping her hands. "I felt so great," she says. "He was coming home." When she first saw him leaving the shuttle, he waved at her. "Oh, that's him," she thought. Later, they met.

"Hi, Mom," the astronaut smiled.

"Oh, you're back!" she answered.

"Yeah."

"Did you have a nice trip?" she asked him.

"Yeah."

Spending the last three days travelling around the world forty-eight times "ain't no beeg ting" to local folks.

"Thumbs up" for Discovery. OVERLEAF: The Westar Satellite being retrieved from space by astronauts Dale Gardner and Joe Allen during a Discovery mission in November, 1984. (NASA)

115

CHAPTER EIGHT
When Ellison Comes Flying Home

Columbia returns to the earth for a controlled landing. (NASA)

Kona had never before seen anything like it. A native son was coming home a conquering hero for a whirlwind circuit of parades, banquets, testimonials, school addresses and state dinners, and all the stops were pulled out. Never before had Kona—or Hawaii for that matter—ever produced a true national hero. Our senators and congressmen had gained prominence on the national scene as had some of our swimmers such as Buster Crabbe and Duke Kahanamoku. Entertainers Hilo Hattie and Don Ho had become household words wherever *Hawaii Calls* was aired or among Midwestern visitors who had saved for a trip to paradise for years. Jack Lord of *Hawaii Five-0* or Tom Selleck of *Magnum P. I.* had become famous Island transplants often identified with Hawaii through their popular television series. And Hawaii-born *nisei* soldiers in the 442nd Regimental Combat Team and the 100th Infantry had earned unparalleled honors in World War II. But never before had an Island-born boy or girl risen to personal, national recognition through the sheer efforts of his or her skill and determination to risk a life in a feat of adventure. Here was a hero for Hawaii who triumphed in the sky and captured the hearts of his fellow Islanders. Kona loved it.

Lieutenant Colonel Ellison Onizuka (he was promoted just prior to the successful shuttle flight) had the qualities that made him an ideal hero. First there was the boyish charm and charisma that reminded older men and women of their son and younger folks of their brother. He conquered space not as an extraordinary individual, but as someone who had made his dreams come true by hard work and determination. He possessed no outstanding gifts of strength, beauty, intellect or *savoir faire*—he was simply a common man who had braved an uncommon adventure. Heroes are reflections of what most of us would like to be or experience in our own lifetimes but they must also have certain vulnerable qualities: their boyishness lends them an air of innocence, humility and a bit of uncomfortableness in the glare of publicity. Isn't that how we would be in the limelight of fame? Like the earlier flying hero Charles Lindbergh, Ellison Onizuka embodied all these qualities with a winning smile that endeared him to Hawaii.

In his characteristic humility, his newly earned status of "hero" was something he did not relish. "I'm a man," he once told a reporter, "not a hero." But he never tarnished the image that he had suddenly been given, especially for the sake of the next generation. He never complained about the sacrifices he would have to make on his time or personal life to fulfill the speaking engagements or promote the space program. While other astronauts returned to their

Space Shuttle Discovery prepares to land at the Kennedy Space Center's landing facility, November 16, 1984. (NASA)

communities as glorified heroes, Ellison always went beyond the ceremonies to devote his time to sharing his dream with the children. "Is there a school nearby?" he would always ask his NASA coordinator. While other astronauts would schedule ten or fifteen appearances post-flight, "Ellison crammed in ninety," his wife Lorna observes. "He exceeded anyone else's post-flight appearances. He was tired, but he kept going. It was the only way he could say thank you. That seemed real important to him." And he always made new friends. When NASA sent him to Seattle for a preflight publicity appearance, he won the hearts of the community. Every summer after, he would be invited and attend Seattle's famous Salmon Fishing Tournament.

It had been nearly six years since the Onizukas had been able to get home to Hawaii and, even before *Discovery* touched earth, preparations were envisioned to roll out the carpet for his triumphant return to Kona. "All the plans are made," declared Kona businessman Fred Fujimoto, "we're just waiting for the date." Tributes and congratulations were already pouring in to Houston from his hometown. An elated Bill Knutson, president of the Kohala-Kona Chamber of Commerce, declared that "We are counting the days when Ellison will return home. We'll have a parade." At Kainaliu, the owner of Kimura Store, Hisashi Kimura, announced that "I'm so proud. He represented not only Kona, but the whole State of Hawaii." Tsuneo Akiyama, president of the Japanese Chamber of Commerce and Industry of Hawaii, proclaimed Ellison's flight as "a feather in the cap for Hawaii." In Washington, D.C., Senator Daniel Inouye was described by an aide as being "very pleased at the achievement" of the Hawaii-born astronaut. Although he had planned to attend the launch, the cold-weather delay had made it impossible. The Big Island's *Tribune-Herald* editorialized that "even those who did not know him growing up in Kona can identify with him and feel good about his accomplishment. For many, his dream come true is our dream come true, too." Council Chairman Stephen Yamashiro of the County Council announced that "we are very happy one of our people on the Big Island has managed to serve his country in such a notable fashion."

In Holualoa, Norman Sakata had his own private thoughts concerning the successful landing of his former explorer scout. Following Ellison's selection as an astronaut, the two men renewed correspondence and a friendship that in the last decade had been quietly put aside. Ellison impressed his former scoutmaster with the care he took in writing articulate, inspiring letters to his fellow scouts admonishing them to dream their dreams and to always "Be Prepared." His humility and his thoughtfulness captured the loyalty of this man

The crew of STS-51C depart the Discovery after their successful DOD mission. (NASA)

who had helped to shape the youth's early confidence and drive. He always showed respect to his elders even after his fame. When he addressed his former scoutmaster as "Mr. Sakata," he was admonished to call him "Norman." "No," Ellison replied, "it will always be 'Mr. Sakata.'"

It was Norman Sakata who had conceived the idea of the twelve-foot scroll and had mailed it to Ellison as a tribute of Kona support. Watching the young astronaut on television descending the shuttle stairs after landing, "I had tears in my eyes. I really rolled tears. I was so proud and it touched me so much." As he told reporters, the ebullient Sakata was "real, real proud when he was selected, and proud when he went up, and now I'm even prouder."

The Kona welcome home parade had been planned for the afternoon of Saturday, March 9, 1985. Ellison, Lorna and their two daughters were to arrive at the Kona-Keahole airport at 3:10 p.m. and then be driven to Kailua Village for a parade through the heart of the town. Unfortunately, poor weather in Houston delayed the flight home and the Onizukas did not arrive until nearly 7:00 p.m. that evening. The parade was canceled and the astronaut and his family were taken directly to the Kona Surf Hotel for a dinner that had been planned in his honor. Over 1,000 Kona residents cheered their astronaut when

he arrived tired but smiling at 8:00 p.m. Jean Ariyoshi, standing in for her husband Governor Ariyoshi, lauded Ellison as "a true son of Hawaii. Although of another generation, he carries on the tradition of those that preceded him. Hawaii has revered its pioneers since the Polynesians in their canoes, and Lieutenant Colonel Onizuka and his colleagues are pioneers in a very special way." Hawaii Mayor Dante Carpenter added that all of Hawaii should celebrate "this native son who has demonstrated through his career and achievement that the sky is not always the limit in relation to our potential, our dreams or our aspirations."

When Ellison took the podium, he evoked a theme of *okage same de*, "I am what I am because of you," which genuinely reflected his gratitude and faith in the people of Kona. "It is great to be home where it all started. You've always made this home for me. When I left Kona for college, I never dreamed I'd return to a celebration. You are wonderful people. Hawaii *no ka oi*." He thanked them for their support and their prayers which had sustained him in his time of need. "The folks back home were always hanging in there. If best wishes could launch a space shuttle, we would have launched in November of '83."

He also took the opportunity, as he always did, to laud the space program and arouse support for further space exploration. "The space shuttle is the most advanced spacecraft that ever orbited Earth. It puts our country in the forefront of space explorations. It makes the United States second to none. The space program has improved our lives, from communications to everyday household items." By 1990 he envisioned that man will possibly "revisit and mine the moon, or possibly a mission to Mars." His patriotism shone through. "I'm proud to have been part of the mission," he said. "I'm proud to have had the opportunity to serve the country in that capacity."

He also spoke of the beauty of earth from space. "The sight and beauty of earth is breathtaking from space. It was fun being weightless and to see the challenge of a new frontier and its potential that must be met. Our state, this island and Kona are a beautiful sight from space. Thoughts of home and all you beautiful people crossed my mind. I wish I had that (the sight) to share with you. Hawaiian music was played from space as the shuttle crossed over the Hawaiian chain." In closing, he said, "It was my first mission and also yours. I'd like to dedicate my first mission to the people of the State of Hawaii. I thank you all for being there when I needed it the most." The crowd cheered their approval.

The March visit was very short. In one week Ellison was slated to visit Konawaena Intermediate and High School, and Kealakehe Elementary, the successor to Honokohau School which had been sold to a church and was now a private school. By Friday the Onizukas would return to their home in Houston, although Ellison promised to return in April for a statewide tour. Coming home to Hawaii was especially important, Ellison believed, for his children. The Houston Meadow Green community was as tightly knit as mauka Kona, but he felt that they should never be too separated from the Island spirit that had shaped both he and Lorna. After five years of separation, the girls had forgotten the style and mannerisms of Kona life. "I kind of fit in," Janelle confessed, "but I don't." It was especially evident in their mainland style of speech—they had even picked up a slight Texas accent. "My Dad got me *Pidgin to Da Max*," the popular local publication with a humorous lexicon of pidgin English terms. "I couldn't pronounce half the words. If I used them on the mainland, they'd of laughed at me." Both Ellison and Lorna spoke clear and articulate standard English. But at home, they could let the pidgin roll out. They did not want the girls to ever feel too much like they were *kotonks* or mainland-style Japanese Americans.

OPPOSITE TOP AND BOTTOM: A *welcome home party in Houston following the return of Discovery. (Onizuka Family)* BELOW: *Secretary of Defense Casper Weinberger congratulates the crew of Discovery for their service to the Department of Defense. (NASA)*

ABOVE: *Ellison thanks the Kona community for their support after his return in March, 1985.* RIGHT: *Ellison presents an official NASA photograph of the Discovery Flight STS-51C to Mrs. Jean Ariyoshi, March, 1985.*

The April tour was another whirlwind. The first visit, Ellison had only one hour to spend at home alone with his mother. On the second visit, he would only have twenty minutes. From arrival to departure, NASA, in cooperation with the Kona planning committee, filled his time with public appearances. The coordinator in Hawaii was Fred Fujimoto, vice president of Hawaii Planing Mill, Ltd. and the brother of Robert Fujimoto, well-known Hilo businessman. A quiet, older *sansei* with a gentlemanly manner that embodies a local spirit, Fujimoto was the son of a well-educated *nisei* businessman. In the Twenties and Thirties his father had built up the successful Hilo-based Hawaii Planing Mill, Ltd., a building supply company which his sons would later head and expand to Kona. During the war, Fred served in the 232nd Engineering Company of the 442nd Regimental Combat Team and in the postwar years, settled with his wife, Midori, in Kona.

Although Fred was aware of the Onizuka family and store, he was not personally involved with them in the Sixties or Seventies. Shirley, Ellison's sister, worked for his company and evidently so had Ellison during one of his summer months at home from college. He never really got to know Ellison. In fact, even after Ellison was selected as a NASA astronaut he was too busy with his own affairs to be too interested. "I thought this is good for Hawaii," he now recalls, "but I didn't get involved in anything for him." That changed in August of 1980. Fred and Midori decided to attend the reunion of the 36th Infantry in Dallas, to which the 442nd Regimental Combat Team was invited due to their spectacular rescue of the Lost Texas Battalion during the war. The reunion was on August 31, 1980 and the Fujimotos decided to also visit Kona's favorite astronaut in Houston. Letters were exchanged, preparations made and the Fujimotos and Onizukas had dinner together. They toured the space center in Houston and Fred remembers starting to get interested in NASA and Ellison Onizuka. In September of 1984, Fred and Midori returned to Houston and also Cape Canaveral at the invitation of Ellison. The friendship and interest blossomed.

In January, 1985 Midori was invited by Ellison to attend his first launch. Fred, who had become friends with Claude, volunteered to chair the testimonial dinner they planned for March. At home in Kona, Fred watched the lift-off, never thinking about the danger but only pleased at the wonderful accomplishment of his young friend. Later Ellison would confide in Fred some of the dangers involved in space travel. "What in the hell are you doing this for then," Fred asked. "I am committed to this," he answered. "It was my own decision and I am going to see this thing through." That convinced Fred that this man had made up his mind and no one was going to change it. "If that's what he wanted, okay let him have it," he thought to himself. Fred Fujimoto was fully involved now in the life of Ellison Onizuka, shouldering all the responsibility for his return celebration. "You are like a second father to Ellison," Mrs. Onizuka once confided to Fred. Never before had the Kona businessman felt more honored or moved.

The itinerary NASA staff coordinator Evelyn L. Thames and Fred planned for Ellison reads like an endless stream of speeches, changing clothes, car rides and cold hotel dinners. Fred conscientiously drove over the Honolulu route time and time again to make sure he wouldn't get lost when escorting Hawaii's astronaut to all the important events. Ellison arrived at Honolulu airport on Wednesday, April 10 where he was greeted by Governor Ariyoshi, Lieutenant Governor and Mrs. John Waihee and official greetings by representatives of the Hawaii Visitors Bureau. The next day he would make speeches at the Department of Education, the Honolulu City Council, the State Capitol, and the Honolulu Pacific Federal Executive Board Federal Week Awards Luncheon, would be interviewed by KGU Talk-Radio and he would give an evening address to the Japan America Society of Honolulu. He would have sometimes only fifteen minutes to go from one ceremony to the next. The

Kona's own cartoonist, Harry Lyons caricatures Kona's own astronaut.

125

next two days in Honolulu were no less hectic with interviews by KHON-TV, KGMB-TV and KSSK Radio, presentations at the Bishop Museum, the Downtown Exchange Club, the University of Hawaii, the Boy Scouts of America and dinner at Washington Place with Governor Ariyoshi, Lieutenant Governor Waihee, Senators Matsunaga and Inouye, Speaker of the House Henry Peters and the Onizuka clan, including Fred Fujimoto. It was a gracious state dinner, but the Governor made Ellison's mother feel especially comfortable by talking about his parents and his father's making of tofu.

Governor Ariyoshi had taken an immediate liking to Ellison. He was struck by the down-home humbleness and modesty of the young Air Force officer who had made such a name for himself. He was most impressed by the astronaut's dedication to the future of Hawaii and especially the planet. Space travel had matured Ellison. Lorna had noted how quiet he could be after the experience. Although his eyes and expressions showed rapture, there was also a deep, almost metaphysical peace that pervaded him. The Governor sensed that futuristic, philosophical attitude in the short discussions they had together. "We talked about Hawaii, the future of our Islands and how important water was to

OPPOSITE TOP, LEFT AND ABOVE: The Hero's Return—Ellison with the children of Hawaii, following his first triumphant space flight, April 1985. (Onizuka Family)

126

our future," the Governor reveals. "He was happy about some of the things we were planning with ocean research. 'So much of the earth is water,' he told me. 'As you move away from the earth you see how much of it is water.'" Ellison stressed to the Governor the shrinking size of the globe through communication and the idea that through space travel, we were becoming a global village. As his mother recalls, Ellison had also told her of his deep impression by seeing how green Hawaii looked from space and how barren the impoverished, famine-ridden desert of Ethiopia. "There are no divisions on earth from space," Claude recalls Ellison having told him.

The Governor and Ellison also played golf together. At the Honolulu International Country Club they played a full round of golf, Ellison confessing that his game was rusty due to the lack of time for practice. During the game, the discussion turned to politics; should Ellison consider a political career once he retired from NASA? He had been courted already for political office. The Governor remembers telling him that politics might not be for him. "Do what you are best suited for," he told the astronaut. "People have different expertise and different things to contribute."

On Monday, April 15 Ellison devoted himself to his favorite post-flight activity: speaking to schools. Manoa, Hanahauoli and Palisades Elementary Schools and Moanalua High School received visits from the Hawaii astronaut dressed in his blue jump suit with the NASA insignias. The next day he flew to Kauai for a series of visits to schools and the crew at the Barking Sands Naval Base. A Maui visit followed on Thursday where he stopped at schools, the Hale Mahaolu Nursing Home, where he spoke briefly in his halting Japanese, and a boy scout/girl scout meeting. By Friday he had returned to Hilo for a string of presentations by the Circumnavigator's Club, the Hawaii Island Chamber of Commerce, the Annual Boy Scout Makahiki, the Boys Club of Hilo, the Hawaii Dental Association, the Kumamoto Prefecture Community Association, the Rotary Club, the Exchange Club, the Lions Club and Aviation Club in Waimea, the Kona Japanese Civic Association and the Governor's Conference on Education. In addition there were the constant visits to schools, especially the elementary schools where the children pressed to be near him, to touch him to make sure he was real and get his signature on even the flimsiest napkin. The children loved him and, in return, he shared all of himself with them.

Usually he was expected at all these events to make an address from a formal speech written for him by NASA. But in most cases, he spoke contemporaneously, from the heart. Especially with the children he stressed simple

128

virtues, the value of education, the excitement of space travel and their dreams for the future. They asked him all kinds of questions. Was he ever scared? ("Things began to happen so fast that there was not time to be scared. It is a hazardous job, but I feel the challenges are worth the hazards.") "How did you sleep?" ("For two nights I slept in a sleeping bag attached to the wall of the *Discovery* and one night just floating freely. And that was the best night's sleep I had while in space.") And the most popular question, "How did you go to the bathroom?" ("There were some problems with the vacuum toilets in the early flights, but those have been cleared up.")

Why did he spend so much time with the children? "I feel they are at an impressionable age and I feel they have the opportunities before them," he told reporters after speaking to a group of Kona school children. In one memorable photograph, Ellison, bedecked in leis, stands among a crowd of children, waving out to the camera and the gleeful kids pack in next to their famous astronaut hero, many waving and others giving the Island "shaka" sign. They had touched a bit of history and he was clearly in his element.

He told the children to believe in their dreams and to strive to do their best no matter what their goals. It was a theme he had once expressed with eloquence to the graduating Class of '80 at Konawaena High School. At that time and time and time again, he inspired his youthful audiences with the challenge of making the world a better place to live through their unswerving commitments to achievement:

> *If I can impress on you only one idea tonight, let it be that the people who make this world run, whose lives can be termed successful, whose names will go down in the history books, are not the cynics, the critics, or the armchair quarterbacks.*
>
> *They are the adventurists, the explorers, and doers of this world. When they see a wrong or a problem, they do something about it. When they see a vacant place in our knowledge, they work to fill that void.*
>
> *Rather than leaning back and criticizing how things are, they work to make things the way they should be. They are the aggressive, the self-starters, the innovative, and the imaginative of this world.*
>
> *Every generation has the obligation to free men's minds for a look at new worlds...to look out from a higher plateau than the last generation.*
>
> *Your vision is not limited by what your eye can see, but by what your mind can imagine. Many things that you take for granted were considered unrealistic dreams by previous generations. If you accept these past accomplishments as commonplace then think of the new horizons that you can explore.*

"He never lost his country roots."

Governor George Ariyoshi was interviewed in his private office at the State Capitol. He had met Ellison Onizuka on several occasions, golfed with the young astronaut and hosted a dinner at Washington Place for Ellison, his family and friends. The two men developed an easy and comfortable rapport with one another.

❝ *What impressed me most about Ellison, was how he went to NASA a country boy and how he remained a country boy. And I mean country boy in the very finest sense. All the values of the community were instilled in Ellison: down-to-earth, a feeling of respect for people where everyone knows everyone else and cares about each other. It was something Ellison communicated. He never lost his country roots.*

One of the things he always wanted to know—was there a school nearby open? He recognized his capacity to touch young people, to inspire young people. In this country of opportunity you could become something. I would consider him a great patriot. He had a great love for his country, a country that gave him the opportunity. He wanted others to know what kind of country this was. I developed a great admiration for him. ❞

From your vantage point, your education and imagination will carry you to places which we won't believe possible.

Make your life count—and the world will be a better place because you tried.

The obligation he felt to give that message to the future generations, to inspire them the way his own *issei* and *nisei* descendants had inspired him, was Ellison Onizuka's one obsession. At the schools, Fred and Evelyn Thames would keep pointing to the clock for Ellison to hurry up. They would be late for the next appointment. Schools were waiting. At one point Fred even threatened to make Ellison chauffeur himself around. "We couldn't get Ellison out of the

schools," Fred remembers. But they realized it was a losing proposition and stopped nagging him about the itinerary and did their best to accommodate the young man who would sign over five hundred signatures at one stop so that every child had his autograph.

On the last day of the exhausting tour, Fred and Ellison drove down to South Point to Naalehu Elementary School, to visit Lorna's parents and give a speech to the children. They had wanted them to stay for lunch, but Ellison had an airplane to catch and he hadn't even had time at home with his mother. So they made a bento lunch for them and Fred and Ellison drove back up to Kona. Along the way, Ellison asked Fred to try and find a house where an elderly Japanese gentleman, Mr. Rakuzo Okinaga, lived who was an old family friend. Fred kept reminding him of the time, but Ellison insisted he needed to visit Mr. Okinaga, the man who was a semi-invalid. He finally found the house and met briefly with the old family friend who was confined to a wheelchair. Mr. Okinaga was elated that the famous Kona astronaut had taken the time to visit him and still remembered so much about him from his childhood. Ellison's next stop was at Kona Hospital where his aunt, Mrs. Tsuruko Katoku, was confined with a heart ailment. She was to pass away two months later.

By the time they got to Keopu, there were only twenty minutes left to visit with his mother. They sat briefly in Fred's car before he had to be taken to the airport. Ellison had already been assigned for another mission even before he landed from STS-51C. As always, he wanted his mother to be there. She was puzzled when she learned about his assignment even as he was flying above the earth. "How did they know he would do a good job until he got back," she asked. "How could they do that? I said to myself if they assign him all the time like that, I can't keep going to Florida." But she reassured her son that if he wanted her at the launch, then she would be there.

The year 1985 had been quite a year for Ellison Onizuka—a year of fulfillment, triumph, achievement and celebration. As his brother-in-law George Matsuoka intimates, when good things happened to Ellison, they flooded in on him. On April 23, after his brief visit with his mother, he ended his nearly two week stint as the conquering hero. He was both exhausted and overwhelmed. He looked forward to getting home to Lorna and the children and to resume his training for his second shuttle flight. It was going to be a special voyage to the stars for Ellison—it was not a classified flight. The date and circumstances of the flight had not yet been finalized, but he was excited and anxious to get back into space. For when he came home the second time, he would be able to tell the children everything.

A Nation bestows its honors on the Kona Astronaut. OPPOSITE: (top) Astronaut Observer Wings; (middle) Senior Space Badge; (bottom) various NASA & Air Force Commendation Ribbons. ABOVE: NASA Secret Mission Medal. OVERLEAF: The nerve center of a shuttle mission—flight controllers in Johnson Space Center's Mission Control Room monitoring the re-entry of a shuttle orbiter. (NASA)

CHAPTER NINE
Challenger: The All-American Space Shuttle

Preparing to leave after an abortive first liftoff attempt, the disappointed but radiant Challenger crew of Flight 51-L is assembled inside the entry gantry of launch pad 39-B, Kennedy Space Center. (NASA)

The crew of *Challenger* flight 51-L seemed to have been carefully chosen to reflect the spirit of America. All walks of life, backgrounds and regions were to be represented on this shuttle flight —civilians and military personnel, five men and two women, four with previous space flight experience. There were to be a Black American and an Asian American on board; Protestants, a Catholic, a Buddhist and a Jew. Their ages ranged from forty-six years old to thirty-five; there was one mother on board, four fathers, one grandfather and a divorcee. They had been raised in a humid Kona coffee field, a small North Carolina fishing village nestled on the Atlantic coast, a rugged mountain community at the base of Mt. Rainier in Washington, in a sweltering tobacco town in the farmlands of South Carolina, the suburbs of upstate New York, the quiet granite New England countryside of Massachusetts and the upper-middle class suburbs of Akron, Ohio.

It was not fate alone that had selected Commander Francis R. (Dick) Scobee, copilot Michael Smith, Mission Specialists Ellison Onizuka, Ron McNair and Judith Resnik, Payload Specialist Gregory Jarvis and teacher Christa McAuliffe for the *Challenger*. Each in their own way had chosen a path that lead to space discovery. They combined a startling spirit of determination and desire that oftentimes compensated for their failings and inabilities as human beings. As children, most of them had harbored private fantasies about space and were fascinated by each successive step as manned flights became a reality. As adults, they either "quietly maneuvered" themselves into a position where becoming an astronaut was possible or leaped at the opportunity when luck and circumstance so determined. They all shared with Ellison Onizuka a compelling commonplaceness which was to make their tragedy all that more painful.

They each, of course, walked a different path to *Challenger*. While Ellison was still in "small kid time," falling off his bicycle in Kona, Dick Scobee was already a teenager growing up in the shadow of Washington's majestic Mt. Rainier in the village of Auburn. He was born May 19, 1939 and was thus the senior astronaut in age and rank. A tall (six foot one inch), strongly built man with a confident, quiet and self-effacing manner, Commander Scobee had logged 6,500 hours of flight time in his long career with the Air Force. A graduate of the Air Force's Moody Air Force School in Georgia, the young Scobee had early on displayed a methodical, conservative style as a pilot— instead of opting for assignment as a jet fighter, he chose the larger C-141 or "trash haulers" as they were derogatorily called by fighter pilots—the large cargo

BELOW: The official NASA patch of Challenger Flight 51-L. RIGHT: Captain Dick Scobee. (NASA)

jets were workhorses, carrying men, weapons, trucks and other supplies. It was an unromantic duty, but reflected the no-nonsense, sober style of this gentle, likeable pilot.

After combat service in Vietnam, Captain Scobee applied for and was accepted to the Test Pilot School at Edwards Air Force Base that Ellison also attended. At thirty-two years of age he was the "old man" to the other men, but was selected to test a variety of experimental aircraft including the X-24B which was designed to be a forerunner of the shuttle. It was a wingless device with rounded contours that would glide back to earth at sharp angles to land safely on earth. Captain Scobee successfully completed two tests of the X-24B, landing the device safely in the desert. When the opportunity to join NASA was announced, Scobee had also applied and was accepted for the shuttle program. He had submitted his application, he told his wife, "on a lark," but he was anxious to be accepted. As he explained in a television interview, "When I was a test pilot at Edwards it was kind of a logical progression in my career and it was one of those things that happened at the right place, at the right time."

On April 6, 1984 Captain Scobee flew the *Challenger's* flight 41-C, a highly celebrated week-long flight that retrieved and repaired the Solar Maximum

Mission satellite. The experience was exhilarating as it is for most astronauts and Scobee was anxious to go again. He had become a grandfather in 1985, but his age did not impair his desires. "We're all doing handstands, yelling, 'Take me! take me!'" he once told an audience. His chance came again when he was selected to be the commander of the *Challenger's* tenth voyage and the twenty-fourth shuttle mission.

His co-pilot was to be Michael J. Smith, a former Navy pilot who had grown up in the fishing village of Beaufort, North Carolina dreaming of flying airplanes. In high school he had been a winning athlete active in football and baseball. He was voted by his classmates at graduation as the "most outstanding" student and possessor of the best physique. His heart was in aviation and he landed an appointment to the Annapolis Naval Academy. After graduation he underwent six years of naval flight training, served on the aircraft carrier USS *Kitty Hawk* in the Vietnam War and later was a jet pilot instructor. As a fighter pilot, he had come to appreciate the risk of flying, but also the thrill. As he told one reporter he selected the Navy over the Air Force because "I thought I might like to fly off aircraft carriers rather than off runways."

In 1977 he applied to NASA for an appointment as an astronaut. His desire to fly had often been expanded to space travel—he kept the large banner headlines when Armstrong walked on the moon and he dreamed of the adventure of launch. When he was turned down for acceptance to the Class of '78, he was disappointed but undeterred. In May of 1980 NASA announced a new round of applications and the Navy officer was selected for the shuttle program. His friends teased him about his assignment as co-pilot for the large, cumbersome orbiter. "You'll do a little flyin' on the way there, a little on the way back, but you won't be flyin' that thing," one friend chided him. "You've got to be crazy, going up there with a Roman candle strapped to your butt." But as he would respond then and time again, to his wife and three children, the danger was minimal. "It's just as safe as getting in any other airplane and flying," he would say.

Judith Resnik had the confidence in herself and NASA to also believe that the complex shuttle system was fundamentally safe. She had first flown into space as a mission specialist on June 26, 1984 aboard the shuttle *Discovery*. At T-minus four seconds before her first scheduled flight, a large explosion and fire erupted at the back of *Discovery*, causing a launch abort and two day postponement to June 26. No one was hurt as investigation revealed that a fuel valve had faltered and the shuttle system automatically aborted. "I was disappointed," Resnik said of the delay, "but I was relieved that the safety systems

Co-pilot Michael J. Smith. (NASA)

do work. It was unfortunate that we had to check them out. But it built a confidence in the whole system."

The young Jewish girl from the suburbs of Akron, Ohio had grown up with more than enough confidence to spare. She had been an excellent student in school, excelling in math and was an accomplished pianist. Choosing for herself a career in science and research, she received a doctorate in electrical engineering at the Carnegie Institute of Technology in Pittsburgh and received a fellow in biomedical research. Often one of few women among a score of men, she learned to be capable, determined and maintained a sense of self-defense. At times she could be officious, formal and distant. She had been married early in the 70's but was now divorced. She dated some of her fellow astronauts and was often teased for her highly public crush on the actor Tom Selleck. She sent him an invitation to watch the lift-off of *Challenger* but he was unable to attend.

In January 1978 she learned that her application as a mission specialist astronaut had been accepted by NASA. She had heard that the agency was looking for scientists and women and she felt confident she would get accepted. She told her father, "Daddy, I'm going to try to be an astronaut," after the application went in. "Good," he told her, "because you're going to get it." With the completion of her first space flight, she would be the second woman in space after Sally Ride's landmark feat in June 1983. She was not disappointed in being number two—"I feel that I am very fortunate to be any woman in space, any person in space."

Ellison Onizuka, Judith Resnik and Ron McNair saw themselves first as professional scientists, engineers and astronauts, and second as Asian American, female and Black American. Ron McNair had also been selected to be one of the Class of '78 and one of the first three Black astronauts. The responsibility of being a role model to young blacks across the nation was a duty that McNair assumed as enthusiastically and devotedly as Ellison did for the children of Hawaii. Young Ron had known all the vicissitudes of poverty and racism growing up in his native town of Lake City, South Carolina. A southern tobacco town inherits a heritage of racial separation and a young, intelligent black child growing up in that environment has a challenge of immense proportions. Lake City, McNair recalled was "one of those places where the railroad track right though the middle of town drew a color line. There was not very much for black kids to do during the summer vacations except go to the field." While Ellison picked coffee, Ron picked cotton, tobacco, beans and cucumbers, worked as a delivery boy and was kept "in his place."

Mission Specialist Judith Resnik in flight during Discovery Mission 41-D. (NASA)

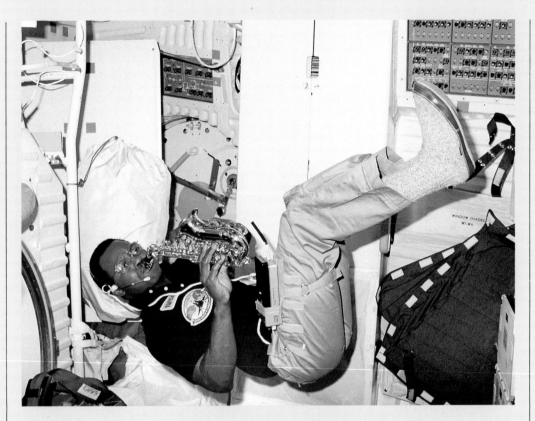

"Somehow it seems these situations never end," he observed. "It's always somebody trying to get in the way. Always somebody trying to limit us."

But they could not limit Ron McNair. Eager for learning and a perfectionist in all he did, he rose to the very heights of the academic world, gaining a scholarship to the Massachusetts Institute of Technology. At MIT he earned his doctorate at the age of twenty-three studying laser physics and was hired at the Hughes Research Laboratories in California. He was working as a scientific researcher at the Malibu facilities when he applied for and was accepted to the shuttle program. He had been fascinated by space travel as a child, had desired to excel as a mission specialists but was, as his brother believed, motivated by a deep sense of curiosity about the workings of the universe. "His fascination was not with space," his brother Eric McNair once commented, "but a fascination in finding out why things happen as they do."

McNair's first space flight was aboard the *Challenger* on February 3, 1984. During the experience he was responsible for working as a team within the orbiter while two of the astronauts floated in space without tethers. It was the first mission in which men flew free in space and mission specialist McNair thus helped paved the way for future experiments of satellite and orbiter repair. It was not long after his return to earth that he was yearning for a new

LEFT: Mission Specialist Ron McNair playing the first musical instrument in space, a saxaphone, on Mission 41-B. (NASA)
BELOW: Co-pilot Smith and Mission Specialists Onizuka and Resnik undergo training for Flight 51-L. (NASA)

Flanked by Teacher-in-Space alternate Barbara Morgan and primary Christa McAuliffe, Payload Specialist Gregory Jarvis is demonstrating the fluid dynamics experiment to be conducted on Flight 51-L. (NASA)

assignment to a shuttle mission. "I was just born to be up there," he told a friend. He could not wait to get back up.

Greg Jarvis, an engineer with Hughes Aircraft and unlikely candidate for becoming an astronaut, had waited so long for space travel that he did not even consider it an open option. As an aerospace engineer, he had helped to design many of the satellites and orbiters that were now proliferating the skies. NASA had announced to their aerospace contractors that not only would their customers be allowed to put satellites on the orbiter, but would allow a payload specialist from the company to accompany the product. Hughes Aircraft was offered two slots, one of which was eventually filled by applicant Jarvis.

Born in upstate New York in the town of Mohawk, Greg Jarvis was an aggressive, hard-working achiever who would become known as the Silent Tornado by his co-workers. He attended the State University of New York at Buffalo majoring in physics and engineering. Both he and his wife were physical fitness enthusiasts and ardent bike riders—he was as competitive with his cycling as he was hard-striving in his engineering career. At Hughes Aircraft, his first successful project was the Marisat program, a communication satellite eventually to be used by the Navy. Jarvis specialized in the communication design of satellites and was always a team member known as a "driver." "He drove himself and others," a co-worker remembered.

140

He had never tried to get into the space program before NASA made the offer to Hughes although he had always gotten up to watch the early morning launches of the shuttles. "I never really said anything about it, but I was really interested when things first started," he confided to his wife. "I thought it was really exciting." He looked forward to his first flight which was slated to be aboard Mission 51-D which kept getting postponed. Then, to his great disappointment, Senator Jake Garn (R-Utah) "bumped" Jarvis from the mission and became one of the first politicians in space. Finally he was reassigned to the *Challenger* flight Mission 51-L. "I am so happy to be here," he announced at a press conference after the selection of astronauts for the flight had been made.

Christa McAuliffe was also "happy" to be there. She had been selected out of 11,000 teachers who had applied for the very special honor of being the first ordinary civilian passenger in space. In August of 1984 President Reagan had first announced that a teacher would be chosen as the first private citizen to fly on the space shuttle. Born Christa Corrigan in Framington, Massachusetts, the young, bright student attended Marian High School, a Catholic coeducational school in Boston. It was there that she was to meet her future husband, Steven McAuliffe and was prepared for her liberal arts education at small Framington State College. Her interests were in social studies and the humanities and after graduation and marriage, she became a public school teacher. In 1978 the McAuliffe's moved to Concord, New Hampshire and Christa began teaching as an American History and English teacher at a variety of schools in the area. Since 1982 she had been teaching tenth, eleventh and twelfth-graders courses in economics, law, American history and a course she developed entitled "The American Woman." The McAuliffes were an active, close couple who enjoyed jogging, tennis and volleyball and raised two children.

Her decision to fill out the eleven-page application to NASA to become the first teacher in space was at the last minute. "As a woman," she wrote in the application, "I have been envious of those men who could participate in the space program and who were encouraged to excel in areas of math and science." She had been impressed by Sally Ride and the other women who were training as astronauts and felt she had seen new opportunities for her students. "I cannot join the space program and restart my life as an astronaut," she continued, "but this opportunity to connect my abilities as an educator with my interests in history and space is a unique opportunity to fulfill my early fantasies. I watched the Space Age being born, and I would like to participate.

NASA selected 114 nominees who were taken to Washington for their final interviews and then to Houston to be given a taste of space travel on the

Teacher-in-Space Christa McAuliffe experiences "weightlessness" in the NASA zero gravity simulator. (NASA) FOLLOWING OVERLEAF: A star voyager floats above the earth. Astronaut Bruce McCandless maneuvers 300 feet away from the orbiter Columbia on the tenth shuttle mission. (NASA)

weightlessness device called the "vomit comet." The risks were discussed so that none of them felt that they would be, as one administrator said, "on any kind of joyride." In mid-July came the announcement from Vice President Bush that Christa had been selected to participate in the shuttle program. The enthusiastic, likeable and confident McAuliffe was the unanimous favorite of NASA. "I would like to humanize the Space Age," she announced "by giving a perspective from a non-astronaut, because I think the students will look at that and say, 'This is an ordinary person'. This ordinary person is contributing to history, and if they can make that connection then they're going to get excited about history, then they're going to get excited about the future. They're going to get excited about space."

It was with this eclectic, diverse cross-section of America that Ellison would join his common fate. At first they did not work together as a squadron team as had characterized the DOD mission. Four of them had been in the Class of '78, but Jarvis and McAuliffe were "non-astronauts," though McAuliffe was careful not to be considered simply a "passenger." Rather than training as a crew, they largely trained individually. McNair had been selected for his background in physics and he was considered crucial for observations of Halley's Comet. Ellison was going to deploy a large communications satellite

ABOVE: *Asian Pacific American Heritage Week plaque honoring Ellison Onizuka, May 10, 1983.* RIGHT: *The wives of Challenger crew Flight 51-L. Left to right, Cheryl McNair, Jane Smith, Marcia Jarvis, June Scobee and Lorna Onizuka. (NASA)*

that would observe the famous comet. "I'll be looking at Halley's Comet," he said at the last news conference before the launch thirty days away. "They tell me I'll have one of the best views around." Resnik would operate the orbiter's pole-like movable arm in the release of a second satellite, the $100 million NASA communications satellite.

McAuliffe would conduct a two part televised "classroom in space" to be broadcast live on the Public Broadcasting System to school children across the nation. Orbiting at 17,500 miles an hour, she was scheduled to take viewers on a tour through the shuttle while in orbit, explaining crew members' roles, showing the location of computers and controls and explaining experiments being conducted on the mission. She would also demonstrate how daily life in space is different from that on earth in the preparation of food, movement, exercise, personal hygiene, sleep and the use of leisure time. The first program was entitled "The Ultimate Field Trip" and the second was intended to show students how one day factories would operate in space. In addition, six film demonstrations of weightlessness, magnetism and other laws of motion would be prepared during flight for distribution to schools following the landing. The *Challenger* was also to carry thirty-two chicken eggs in an experiment by Purdue University sophomore John Vellinger to determine the effects of weightlessness on the unhatched embryo.

In his characteristic style, Ellison spent much of his time assisting other members of the crew in their preparations. He and Mike Smith became close, Smith commenting on the fact that he liked Ellison's "right perspective." In December 1985 they began training as a crew, undergoing simulation testing. Bonds began to grow as the crew accepted their "first teacher" astronaut. In her own style, she baked pies for her fellow crew members and at one publicity photo session, they surprised her by showing up wearing caps, tassels and gowns complete with apples, lunch pails and mascot. Jarvis and McAuliffe became close friends, sharing their "non-astronaut" status and an enthusiasm for bike riding.

The last two years had been hectic for Ellison and whenever he could, he would find peace and relaxation. Being a fishing enthusiast, he would sometimes pack his bento, musubi and beer in a cooler and head out to the Gulf of Mexico to go fishing. Rowing his boat out one time, he realized that he had remembered all the food and beer, but completely forgotten his fishing pole. It made no difference. On the March Koṇa trip, his brother arranged for a fishing expedition with just the family and a few friends. It was intended as a relaxing trip, but Ellison caught his first marlin—a 425 pound giant he would

The Boy Scouts of America present a trophy of appreciation to one of their own.

145

The brothers Onizuka bringing in the "big one," Kona March 1985. (Onizuka Family)

later proudly pose with for photographs. Little Darien was also lucky that day, catching a forty-four pound marlin. What Claude remembers about the trip, though, is that on the way back Ellison fell asleep on a bench. "It was really peaceful for him on that boat," Claude says. "No phone calls, no one around."

Ellison had to work as hard to find time to relax as he did in doing everything else, Lorna now recalls. He did not relax by reading—he used to tease her about the time she spent reading romantic novels. Once she suggested he read *Shogun* but after a few pages he put it down. It was boring, he said, though Lorna stressed that you have to get past the first pages to appreciate a novel. The only television he watched was sports events and they did not go out much to the movies. He maintained his interest in the girls' soccer and studies, and always included them as much as he could in the space program. For example, one afternoon he called home and asked the girls if they had any ideas concerning the patch to be designed for Flight 51-L. Darien thought about it and suggested an apple for the teacher which later appeared beside Christa McAuliffe's name. But his time for his family was admittedly shrinking in direct proportion to the nearing of countdown.

Family events and trips had increasingly been marked by hurried schedules, public appearances and no or little time for family. In 1983, Ellison, Lorna, the children and his mother had flown to Japan for a memorable visit to his ancestral homeland. The itinerary was as busy and pressured as any that he would know during the Hawaii tour after his first flight. NASA had recognized the value of Ellison to building bridges of good will between Japan and the United States and the visit with the Crown Prince and other Japanese dignitaries were handled by Ellison with aplomb. The Japanese seemed as taken by the Onizukas as Hawaii was, though they spoke haltingly in the English language or through an interpreter.

The most moving event for Ellison was his return to the family ancestral village in Minou and the offerings to the Onizuka ancestral tomb. When it was determined he was going to Japan, he had been asked what he wanted to see and he quickly answered the ancestral village. Every time he returned to Kona, he always laid a wreath at his grandparents and father's tomb—it was a natural reaction for the filial son. Since he was unaware of his family genealogy, a Professor Kuroda at Kyushu University assisted in the search for the family tomb. Ads were put in local newspapers seeking descendants with information and they received several replies, one of which led them to the tomb. It was an emotional rendezvous for Ellison. The grandson of Kichihei and Wakano Onizuka had returned home to pay tribute to the spirits of the family. He stood

A Fellow Astronaut Remembers

*Colonel Loren Shriver flew with Ellison Onizuka on his first voyage into space
on the shuttle Discovery. It was a classified Department of Defense flight and both
Ellison and Colonel Shriver had been hesitant to discuss any of the particulars of the
flight. But Colonel Shriver was not reluctant to talk about his close friend and
fellow space voyager after the Punchbowl graveside services held
for Ellison Onizuka on June 2, 1986.*

Ellison with the "big one." (Onizuka Family)

❝ *One of the main qualities possessed by Ellison was that he always had
time for someone else. Giving a hand around his friends' homes in Houston,
or helping someone move or calling a roofing company were common
activities for Ellison. That comes back to the situation in Hawaii.
When things need to get done, the whole community gets involved in it.
He was just that kind of individual. He was very liberal with his time.
He had lots of projects to work on, but he still could find time to help build
a deck in the backyard or to help make a luau. He was also involved in
softball teams and in youth soccer programs. He was extremely interested in
young people, encouraging them to dream and work hard towards dreams.*

*I will remember Ellison as a fellow crew member, who was very much
dedicated to the mission. He had an extremely good sense of humor and
always kept us a little bit comically relieved in a lot of situations. He was a
jolly sort of guy and yet serious in the crew aspect of the mission. He was
actually ideal for a crew mission. He worked very hard at what he was
doing. It's hard to describe those personal feelings you have and mental
glimpses that build up in the mind every now and then about situations in
the simulator and during the three-day flight. Crazy little things come into
your head from time to time. That's just the way it'll be, I guess.
I probably won't forget that.* **❞**

in silent prayer. Lorna secretly picked up a small pebble from the grounds and
put it in her purse. As long as you have something that old and treasured, she
believed, you will never be poor in mind and spirit.

147

He promised his escorts that after his second voyage, he would return to Japan. He thoroughly enjoyed the experience, relished the food, especially the *natto* beans and looked forward to discovering more about his roots. He was impressed that although he wouldn't read the book, one of his own ancestors had been a shogun. Ellison's popularity stretched to other groups of Japanese Americans with whom he made contact. After his triumphant first flight, he was adopted by the Japanese Americans of Los Angeles as one of their own. He was invited to ride in the prestigious Nisei Week parade and was feted by ethnic newspapers and community leaders as a wonderful example for Asian American children throughout the nation.

So even in his travels and "relaxation" breaks, Ellison Onizuka never fully enjoyed the peace or solitude that he must have looked forward to the day in the distant future when he might retire from NASA and return to Hawaii as he had planned. But that day was still very far off. Fred Fujimoto recalls that after a visit to a high level Air Force official, Ellison was asked if he would consider returning to the Air Force. It would have meant the possibility of taking over a command. But he was going to stay with NASA just as long as they would have him, he replied. Considering that NASA already had him scheduled for a third shuttle mission, it seemed unlikely that Ellison Onizuka would soon find rest.

By January the *Challenger* had been readied on launch pad 39B waiting for lift-off. The giant white orbiter was 122 ft. in height and made a remarkable Christmas ornament. Ellison found time to write his last letter to Norman Sakata and the young scouts of Hawaii, one more time congratulating them on their accomplishments and admonishing them to "Be Prepared!" for the future. "The need is great for men who hold high values as 'duty to God and country', and 'duty to others'…and for men who know the true meaning of 'the good turn,'" he wrote. "The first eight words of the scout oath express a philosophy worthy of remembering as we tackle the many tasks and decisions that confront us every day of our lives. 'On my honor I will do my best' has enormous meaning and can exert a potent influence for a meaningful future."

There were other personal preparations for Ellison to attend to. He asked ground control if a decal of the University of Colorado could be placed on the box-like satellite that would be sent out to observe Halley's Comet. They agreed. He also called Lorna to tell her that he had forgotten his University of Colorado class ring. It was a good luck piece when he flew and she agreed to bring it to him. Though the crew was officially in quarantine, he always took the opportunity to reunite with Lorna and the children on the pretext of having forgotten something. Children were not allowed in the quarters due to their highly contagious diseases. He spoke to them on the phone before the flight—he made them laugh and they cried a little. He had asked Claude to bring their Mom to quarantine for dinner. Claude thought it was best not to put Mrs. Onizuka through the rigorous physical exam. "We'll see you in Houston," he told Ellison.

Since this flight was not classified, the number of invitations to family, friends and guests could be increased. Whenever one of the crew members did not use an invitation, Ellison asked to use it. Over sixty Hawaii people had been invited and they flew to Florida. A huge celebration in Houston was being planned after the return of the *Challenger*. Special foods were being shipped to Houston from Kona, including kalua pig, lomi salmon and barbecue meat from Parker Ranch. Representative Akaka could not watch the lift-off, but he happily agreed to be at the luau. By January 21, all the Hawaii delegation had arrived with their huge banner reading ONIZUKA '86. They attended a Saturday brunch the day before the scheduled launch which was hosted by

149

ABOVE AND OPPOSITE: Mrs. Mitsue Onizuka and the Hawaii delegation at the viewing stands of Challenger Flight 51-L. (Onizuka Family) RIGHT: The Challenger crew waves its final farewell. (NASA)

Lorna and Judy Resnik's parents. The Onizuka clan and the Resnik family got to celebrate together the upcoming flight.

But the launch was postponed from Sunday, January 26 to the next day. The astronauts, hoping and preparing for the Sunday launch, missed watching the Superbowl on television. NASA officials were concerned about the threatening weather conditions both in Florida and at the emergency landing strip in Africa. Unacceptable cloud banks were moving in on the cape, though the shuttle had a three-hour "window" for a clear launch. After 52 million

150

miles of safe space voyaging, NASA was stressing that the time schedule was secondary to the safety of the flight.

Monday morning the air was clear and brisk at fourty degrees. The launch was on schedule. The crew boarded the shuttle and as the countdown reached T-minus nine minutes, it was called off. A bolt on the handle of an external hatch was stuck. NASA technicians tried to remove it, but could not. The drill they were using developed a dead battery. Four hours passed as the crew sat in the shuttle, Jarvis grumbling that his leg was going to sleep. When the bolt was finally blown, the weather had become windy and the flight was postponed to Tuesday at 9:38 a.m.

That night Ellison called the hotel to speak to his mother. One of the relatives answered and called Mrs. Onizuka to the phone. She simply said, "Hello."

"Mom, are you here?" he asked.

"Yes, I'm here."

"Thanks for coming," he told her. "How's everything."

"Fine. How are you?"

"Everything is okay," he answered.

"Well," she assured him, "keep yourself healthy. Accomplish your duty well."

"Yes, I'll do that," the son answered. "I'm happy to be going, Mom. Everything will be alright."

She replaced the receiver, confident that her son would be safe. The next morning the crew boarded the *Challenger* at 8:23 a.m. A launch pad technician started to give Christa McAuliffe an apple. "Save it for me and I'll eat it when I get back," she told him. Ellison with the six others strode to the orbiter, smiling and waving. It is an image his mother still prefers to see.

The cold weather had been worse than NASA technicians ever remembered before a launch. The temperatures had dropped to twenty-seven degrees that morning as icicles formed on the launch pad. The cold temperatures and a broken water pipe on the pad delayed the launch to 11:38 a.m. The crew went through pre-flight checks. The countdown reached T-minus ten seconds and then a NASA official announced, "we have main engine start." The *Challenger* thrusted upward, the massive external fuel tank unleashing its fury in a thunderous roar. "*Challenger*, go at throttle up," a voice spoke from Mission Control. Commander Scobee gave the last transmission. "Roger, go at throttle up."

The *Challenger* carried its precious load into the mystery of the future.

OVERLEAF: *The Challenger crew of Flight 51-L. Left to right, Mission Specialist Onizuka, Co-pilot Mike Smith, Teacher-in-Space Christa McAuliffe, Pilot Captain Dick Scobee, Payload Specialist Gregory Jarvis, Mission Specialists Ron McNair and Judith Resnik.* (NASA)

151

EPILOGUE
They Touched the Face of God

Challenger is launched on October 30, 1985 for the twenty-second shuttle mission. (NASA)

Life in Keopu, Kona today is quietly resuming an almost normal pace. In the hectic weeks following the tragedy, friends and well-wishers, television crews and journalists, curious residents and visitors, descended upon the village, offering sympathy and support, looking for news or simply wanting to be a part of a small bit of history. Most of them were solemn—they had been touched by the young Kona boy who had brought such honor and glory to his community while remaining warm and humble. Ellison always spoke from the heart. Some of the reporters who had covered Hawaii's astronaut story from the beginning, found their present chore embarrassingly painful—they had become friends with their subject's easy manner, his off-camera humor and willingness to share. Ellison always had the ability to make people feel at ease and that he really cared about them. Cars drove slowly past the Onizuka store, as if viewing the scene of his boyhood would put them in touch with who Ellison Onizuka had been.

Mrs. Onizuka has reopened the store and spends much of her time stocking the shelves, pricing, finding new room for supplies and sweeping the porch. It's not like the old days, when the kids were small and the Onizuka store was a busy stopover along the Mamalahoa Highway. People shop at supermarkets now. The coastal highway that connects the hotels and the growing suburbs of Kailua-Kona redirected most of the traffic away from mauka Kona. And most everyone has their own telephone, so Mrs. Onizuka is not busy taking messages for her neighbors. Her store though still brings her a little income. She has an electronic buzzer hooked up in the store's entrance so that when she watches television in the back living quarters she will know when a customer walks in. She will rush up to the front counter, share her shy but friendly smile and give a slight bow and a warm hello. The Onizuka store is still a country store. She knows most of the customers by name.

She sweeps her porch talking about her son Ellison, fondly remembering the little boy with candy-stuffed pockets campaigning for local politicans and falling off his bicycle. She proudly points out the mailbox stand across the road that he made one summer before he became a famous astronaut. His daughter had made a crude hand sign warning "Man at Work" while her dad erected the sturdy supports. "It'll last a long time," she stresses. She also talks about Lorna and the grandchildren, worrying for them now that they must put their lives together in Houston without Ellison. She is reassured that their NASA family and community friends have been real kind and helpful to them, but Texas is so far away from the family. She guesses that they will keep their home there as

Memorial services at Punchbowl Cemetery, June 2, 1986. (Dave Davis)

At a near-by viewing stand arranged for NASA guests, Fred and Midori Fujimoto viewed the launch with his brother and sister-in-law, Robert and Alice Fujimoto. When the *Challenger* began to lift, Midori whispered to Fred that "this is funny. It doesn't look like the last time." She thought there was too much smoke. Her husband reassured her that everything must be all right just as the main fuel tank erupted. They were then overwhelmed by the panic and confusion of the audience. The PA system asked everyone to remain calm and return to the buses for transport back to the space center. NASA doctors and nurses checked family members and examined them for shock. Coffee and donuts were given out as the family and friends retreated into a chilling silence. Their love for the man they had just lost was so immense that none could fathom the disaster they had just witnessed. The immediate family was taken to crew quarters and then to Patrick Air Force Base. In the slow motion of time, the Hawaii delegation departed for Houston and then on February 3, they flew home to the Islands.

Hawaii wept for its native son. In their home in Kainaliu, Bill and Bertha Paris watched the launch on televison. When the cameras revealed icicles on the launch pad, Mr. Paris remembers saying to his wife, "What the devil are they doing? I had read that the shuttle doesn't operate well in cold weather. I had a bum feeling." He dozed off before the last countdown, but Bertha woke him up when the explosion occurred. They sat upright in bed on that early Kona morning and refused to believe what they saw. Up the road at the National Guard Armory where Sargeant Matthew Heneralau works, the former explorer adviser to Ellison Onizuka also could not believe the report on the office radio. Friends called him with a shocked, "Hey, you heard about Ellison?" He really would not believe it till he got home to watch it on television. Only with his eyes could he accept what was the impossible— "it was many, many more times worse than an accident. You are part of it. I could not work, not thinking about it."

Kona streets were somber. Folks asked each other if they had heard about Ellison. They shared their special memories. They sent their telegrams and words of love to Houston. A black bow and a maile lei hung on the closed, lonely Onizuka store door.

In Honolulu, Governor Ariyoshi first heard the report of the disaster over his radio. He quickly turned on the television set to watch aghast the video replays of those brief, sixty seconds of flight 51-L. He remembered the country boy who had spoken so eloquently about the future of the planet. In Washington, D.C., his friend Representative Akaka was in disbelief. All activity had stopped on Capitol Hill when word of the *Challenger* tragedy was announced. The space program had been such a wonderful example of the unity of Americans and now these fine young men and women had perished before the unbelieving eyes of millions. Never had such a single, stunning catastrophe been witnessed live by so many people.

In the intervening months the nightmare of that terrible sight has not completely diminished. Memorial services in Houston, Kona, California, Colorado and later at Punchbowl Cemetery gravesite, can never fully heal the void. The winning smile of the star voyager remains with us. He left us also the legacy of his dream.

In his dreams begin our responsibilities. He believed in a world where every creature would fulfill their potential by looking beyond their limitations. He taught the children to look inside themselves to find that spark of dedication to make themselves and their communities a better place in which to live. He envisioned other worlds and adventures so that we could make this earth a more tolerable and peaceful speck of dust in the universe. His dream must not only survive in the monuments we erect or the honors we bestow. It is our responsibility, each in our own private way, to strive to fulfill our destiny with strength, kindness, humility and honor.

His dream does live on in the children. Young Lori is the nine-year-old daughter of Claude Onizuka who is interviewed in her family's living room. Her charming, toothy smile captivates you as she speaks of her Uncle Ellison. It is the Onizuka charisma passed on to the *yonsei* or fourth generation. She attended the first launch in January 1985 and remembers the "white dot with an orange thing on the bottom of it" going far up and away into the sky. "What do you want to be when you are older?" she is asked.

"I want to be an astronaut when I grow up," she brightly and unfearingly answers.

What do you want other children to know about your Uncle Ellison?

"That he was terrific," she replies, without hesitation.

Farewell, Ellison Onizuka. You have given us many memories. Our children have been inspired by your gifts of wisdom and sacrifice. Your dreams have left us much to do. May your adventurous spirit find joy soaring boundless among the stars until that day of reunion when we too shall have "slipped the surly bonds of earth…and touched the face of God."

A squadron's affectionate farewell to Lt. Col. Ellison Onizuka—the Missing Man Formation, June 2, 1986. (Dave Davis)

159

MCNAIR ONIZUKA RESNIK

SCOBEE SMITH

MCAULIFFE JARVIS

They slipped the surly bonds
of earth to touch the face of God

Bill Corey

Written by: Dennis M. Ogawa and
    Glen Grant
Art Direction: Bill Fong
Design: Leo Gonzalez
Design Assistant: Debra Michimoto
Production Artists: Lisa Lindbo and
    Peter Matsukawa

Title Lettering: Leo Gonzalez
Typesetting: Ad Type, Inc.
Text Type: Goudy Old Style and
    Goudy Old Style Italic

This book was printed and bound by
Dai Nippon Printing Co., Ltd., Tokyo, Japan.